Never Tease a Dinosaur

Never Tease

a Dinosaur

BY JOSEPH F. HANNAN

Tales of a man in a woman's world—

told by a male elementary schoolteacher

HOLT, RINEHART AND WINSTON   NEW YORK

LA
2317
.H415
A3

To Margy, whose editorial functions far exceed her matrimonial vows; and to Joe, Kathleen, Frank and Matt for their patient acceptance of the Saturday ban of silence.

KIDS love to draw dinosaurs. One such artist, enthusiastic but uninformed, drew a fierce Tyrannosaurus rex confronting a cowering spear-wielding cave man—an anachronism since old Rex was gone before man even appeared on the scene.

"What's wrong with this picture?" I asked the class.

"That's easy," said seat two, row three. "Never tease a dinosaur."

Contents

The Schoolmarm Needs a Shave

I AM an elementary schoolteacher; a male elementary schoolteacher; a dedicated, hard-working, shave-twice-a-day male elementary schoolteacher. Yet at least one-quarter of the notes I receive from parents are addressed to MRS. Hannan. If called to their attention the writers laugh and say, "Well, I'm so used to women teachers, you know."

All textbooks, teacher's manuals, magazine and newspaper articles always refer to the teacher as *she*. (You'll notice in this book that I switch back and forth. I don't feel well enough established yet to go all out for *he*.)

Lavatory facilities in the older schools are apt to be marked BOYS, GIRLS, or LADIES, never MEN. Some aren't marked at all, they're community property. A man using one of these has a distinct feeling of insecurity, his welcome never having been clearly established.

At the local tavern, where you have been accepted as a flashy if somewhat erratic pool player, the discovery that you teach elementary school always leads to, "You don't mean to tell me you're a schoolteacher!" The intimation being that a pool player couldn't possibly be a good teacher. I become angry and it is immediately apparent by my flashing eyes and the vulgarity of my reply, "What the hell's wrong with teaching school?"

Somewhat taken aback by my ill-tempered response the questioner will try to placate me. "Gee, I'm sorry, buddy, it's just that you don't think of a big guy with those little . . ." Here his voice trails off in deference to the sparks from my glance, and he moves off to join a more congenial companion.

He could have been worse. He could very well have been the other bird, who, in response to my statement that I teach elementary school, becomes very solicitous, pats me on the back, and says, "Gee, that's too bad, but maybe after a couple of years you'll work your way up to high school."

Through clenched teeth I inform him that I'm not interested in "working my way up," that elementary school is a field in itself, that I had to have special training to teach in elementary school, and that I am happy dealing with "little kids."

But it's not all darkness for the male teacher in elementary school. Let me show you the advantages of the situation. An irate father writes you a note addressed to MRS. Hannan as follows:

> I'm sick of you picking on my kid. I've had trouble with your type before. I'm coming in tomorrow and we'll get this straightened out once and for all.

The next day on the playground he strides up to you, jaw out-thrust, and says, "I'm looking for MRS. Hannan. They said she'd be out here."

"I'm MR. Hannan," you reply, punching a forefinger into his chest, "and I want to tell you about that darn kid of yours. He's bugged me for the last time. Either you take care of him at home or I'll corner him in a dark alley and paddle him good." The unexpected gender and the aggressive attitude will bring him around to your way of thinking in no time.

Of course, the next time he will not be as susceptible to aggressiveness, so perhaps you'd better leave him under friendly circumstances. To do this use a one-two punch: One—Get him to agree his boy's a problem. If you do this right he'll give you written permission to box the kid's ears.

4

Two—Ask him what he does for a living, then tell him you worked at that for years while you were attending college. The result is known as rapport.

One other advantage of being a male elementary teacher is the thing I call the Harem Effect. Every man has dreamed of having a number of women dedicated to keeping him happy. Don't get me wrong. Unless you're the Gregory Peck type, no group of women will devote themselves wholeheartedly to your happiness. But you must remember, I didn't say you could have a harem, I just said you will feel the Harem Effect. The Harem Effect is feeling—no, I'll put it another way.

The Harem Effect is a psychological condition set up in the victim's (perhaps subject's would be a better word) mind by being continually surrounded by women.

Women, by instinct, tend to wait on a man. So, while eating lunch they are apt to pour your coffee and select the best piece of cake for you and run to get you a more comfortable chair. In addition, they ask your advice on methods of handling rough boys, the best place to eat, and what that funny noise was that started in their automobile just this morning.

Now the best thing you can do for a man's ego is ask his advice. When the same man is asked by ten or twelve females for advice on countless questions of national and international import, you may well imagine the effect. This man feels like a sultan surrounded by his harem.

Of course, the sultan has a duty to the harem. You will be called upon countless times to perform duties only a man can carry out successfully. For example you will: change flat tires, put on snow chains, unlock locked bumpers, and carry in bulky packages. There may be more than one male in the school. This may lead to conflict and the wise administrator would do well to give some thought to placement. Perhaps if he gave each man so many women to take care of, or perhaps all the women on a single floor. . . . Still, when you get two males together you know how it is. They fight.

Years ago America handed the education of the smaller children over to women. To insure that the ladies would have a monopoly on the work, the pay scale was set so as to eliminate any man with a family to support. It has only been recently that suburbia, frightened by the fact that there is no male influence around the house, because Dad is out running Little League or Boy Scouts, has begun paying men enough to tempt them into elementary school work. Many of the children are seeing a male teacher for the first time. Therefore the teacher must be the epitome of manliness. A woman is allowed to show pain, fear, and perhaps even cry a little. Not so the male who must be the steadfast prototype of good-old-fashioned American manhood.

Let's take three areas in which the pattern of masculinity is set by society.

Pain

It is well to emulate the Indian in complete impassivity when in pain.

For example: If when arising from your desk you smash your knee on an open drawer, do *not* scream, clutch the injured member, or even limp. In a woman any or all of these are perfectly acceptable. A man must stride pridefully away, seemingly unaware that anything has occurred. Perhaps you could stride out into the hall where you can jump, grimace, and perhaps even indulge in a few under-the-breath expletives. But remember, when returning to the classroom, SMILE.

Cold

All teachers are subjected to a condition of torture called (I've never found out why) "court duty." This consists of supervising children during lunch hours, either indoors or out.

During the spring and early fall, this outdoor chore can be quite invigorating. You breathe deeply, smell the new flowering shrubs or admire the red and gold hues of the changing leaves, and all seems right with the teaching profession.

6

But when the temperature drops to 20° the whole mess takes on a bleak appearance. Having been thoroughly chilled by the twenty-five-foot walk from your car to the school that morning you have been fervently praying for an indoor schedule at noon. But at 11:45 the note arrives and your anticipatory smile freezes, the first of many parts to be so affected.

Teachers:
    Since the sun is shining and the mud on the playground has now frozen solid, the children will play outdoors.

Signed,
The Principal

Now female teachers have no real problem. They simply stand in the warm hallway, surpervising through the window, allowing only those children who show obvious signs of frostbite into the building.

Not so the male. Having braggingly described in some detail your rigorous tour of duty in the North Atlantic in mid-winter, you've left yourself no out but the great outdoors.

It is made obvious by the first lung-searing breath that no human can survive one half hour of this duty standing still. You therefore decide to join a game of touch football. Since you're the best passer (you've told them so yourself) the boys elect you to run one of the teams.

You run, dodge, sidestep, pass, ignoring your frozen clawlike hands, congratulating yourself on how quickly time passes when one keeps busy. And pass it does. In the interminable time you've been out in this thirty-mile gale, five whole minutes have slipped away.

You excuse yourself, handing over the ball to another quarterback (one with gloves), murmur something about ". . . you fellows need the practice more than I do," and retire to a protected cranny away from the wind, where, in a few minutes, the girls from your class find you.

"Are you cold, Mr. Hannan?" they ask.

"No," you lie.

"Then how come you're shivering?"

"Well, you see, girls, during the last war when I was in the Pacific I contracted a bad case of malaria and it often comes back on me causing me to . . ."

That day you eat lunch with the janitor in the boiler room. It's dusty but that old furnace has a warm friendly glow.

Sports

Baseball occupies a most important place in our culture. It behooves anyone who would teach fourth, fifth, or sixth grade boys to have a sound knowledge of the game. Again the women have it easy. No boy expects a *woman* to know about baseball. If she can name the two teams who are playing in the World Series she is considered a good joe and no more is expected of her.

An American male, on the other hand, is per se an expert on baseball. Never mind that during his formative years he spent his time curled up with Montaigne's essays rather than on the nearest sand lot. Now he is teaching boys and to gain their respect must be conversant with the National Pastime. Anything less borders on subversion.

For those who have absolutely no skill in athletics or whose lack of confidence undermines what little they do possess, it may be well to stick to umpiring. This requires only a superficial knowledge of the rules (no need to be too detailed, the kids will notify you if you're wrong) and has the added feature of preserving the dignity of the teacher. Of course it in no way causes the children to respect you. A teacher-umpire will be baited rarely but will never be respected.

The teacher who joins the game AND IS SUCCESSFUL will be respected. The danger is obvious. A costly error might well undermine your whole relationship with those who count—the class athletes.

On the other hand a spectacular play may win them to your side forever. A calculated risk, you say? Perhaps not, if properly planned.

First, take over a crucial position. Let's say left field. Now listen closely. If the ball is hit directly at you, don't catch it. Pretend you've lost it in the sun, that you weren't ready, that your shoe is untied. Whatever you do, don't attempt to catch that ball. The reasoning is obvious. If you drop a ball hit right to you, where's your excuse?

On the other hand, if a ball is hit over your head or in front of you, try for it. If you miss it's an understandable error. If you make the catch, your reputation is made. Two or three such catches should carry you through an entire season.

But no matter how great his courage, how thorough his training, how varied his pre-teaching experiences, one day early in September our teacher will be confronted by his first class.

In addition to his schooling he will have had the advice of other teachers which consists of, "Keep them busy and they won't give you any trouble."

His relatives will have made dire predictions betraying their deep-seated and ofttimes justifiable lack of confidence in his ability. His friends will have made him a present of *The Blackboard Jungle,* which, unfortunately for his peace of mind, he has had time to read.

It's no wonder he starts as the warning bell rings and the clean, well-mannered children begin to file into the room. A look at their anxious-to-please expressions should have settled his nerves immediately, but our teacher is seeing nothing at all. Ashen-faced, he has managed to stand erect by clinging to his desk, which has become his fortress and which, incidentally, hides his trembling knees.

Remembering the admonition to "keep them busy" he plunges into his new task. His voice is a strained croak as he speaks his first words to his class.

"Take out your spelling books."

The children exchange puzzled glances and shift uncomfortably in their seats.

Prepared for such defiance by his reading of *The Blackboard Jungle,* he raises his voice. "You heard me. I'll have no insubordination. Get out your Spelling books!"

Again his orders are met by an uncomfortable shuffling of feet.

Incensed and beginning to panic, he starts to repeat his order for

9

the third time, when one boy, braver than the rest, raises his hand.

"Well," glares our teacher.

"Sir, we don't have any Spelling books, we don't have any books. You didn't give them out yet."

"Oh! Oh!! Well, all right then. Well, well, well [panic is mounting]. Well, everyone write a composition on 'What I Did This Summer.' "

A few children stir but most just sit eying the teacher until the brave boy raises his hand again.

"Sir, we don't have any paper. The teacher usually gives out paper."

"Oh, oh, oh, yes. Here you"—he points to the brave one—"go to the closet, get out a package of paper and give it out."

(He assigns someone to the job because his trembling legs won't carry him as far as the closet.)

As the paper is being distributed to the children a boy and girl enter the room. Anxious to show that he is alert and will tolerate no violation of school rules, he is prompt in his decision, "You two go to the office, you're late." In a few minutes they return bearing a note.

Dear Mr. Hannan:

It is only 5 minutes to 9. School starts at 9 o'clock when the opening bell rings. Please admit these students.

The Principal

At 9:10 our teacher calls a halt to the compositions. "Hey," the kids chorus, "we didn't have time to finish."

"Never mind," he growls, "finish it for homework. Now get out the Arithmetic books."

"Hey," calls the brave boy, "you didn't give us books yet." Now our teacher feels that his authority and judgment are being questioned.

"Listen you," he says, "don't you know better than to call a teacher, 'hey'? Haven't your teachers and parents taught you common politeness? You're to call me by my name, not 'hey.' "

"But sir . . ."

10

"Never mind, go to the office, I know your type. I won't stand for insubordination." As the boy starts to leave the room the class begins to revolt.

In unison they scream, "You never told us your name."

"Well," he snaps right back, "if you weren't so insubordinate I would have told you long ago."

"What's insubordinate?" asks a little girl.

"Be quiet and copy my name."

He writes shakily and slowly and the children start dutifully to copy. "I want that copied one thousand times while I'm giving out books." As our insecure hero stumbles around distributing the forgotten books he sneaks a glance at the clock: 9:35.

"My God, I won't last till noon let alone work at this job for a lifetime," he thinks.

From the corner of his eye he catches a glimpse of a boy rising in his seat, a threatening object in his hand. Turning quickly to face the menace, *Blackboard Jungle* still fresh in his mind, he cries, "DROP IT!"

"Drop what?" asks the boy.

"DROP . . . THAT . . . KNIFE!"

"What knife? I don't got a knife."

"What do you have?"

"It's a pencil, just a pencil."

"Why were you sneaking up behind me with a pencil?"

"I wasn't sneaking up behind you. I was just going to sharpen my pencil. See, the pencil sharpener is over there."

"Well, sharpen your pencil and no back talk. I won't stand for insubordination."

"What's insubordination?" asks a little girl.

"Be quiet and copy my name."

"I finished."

"Then do the first ten pages."

"In what?"

"In every book on your desk. And that goes for everyone else in this class. I won't stand for insubordination."

"What's insubordination?" asks a little girl.

A clanging bell is the final nerve-cracking straw.

"FIRE DRILL," screams our hero rushing aimlessly around. "Everyone remain absolutely calm. No talking! REMAIN CALM! FOLLOW ME! NO TALKING. I WON'T STAND FOR INSUBORDINATION. NO TALKING!"

"Sir," says the brave little boy. "Sir," he says. "Mr. Hannan," he says. "Mr. Hannan, this isn't a fire drill. That's the lunch bell. Don't worry, Mr. Hannan, I'll take the class to the lunchroom. You just go and sit down awhile. I'll see to everything."

"What's insubordination?" asks a little girl.

After lunch the whole character of that class changed. They well knew he wasn't to be trifled with and they got right down to work. In no time at all they organized a system for passing and collecting papers. They reminded him politely that he had forgotten to salute the flag and do morning prayers that day. They told him that this was required by state law and offered to set up a rotating system to relieve him of this administrative responsibility. They explained about the attendance sheet and how important it was to keep it accurately. Fire and air raid drill procedures were carefully outlined to him. They also taught him to admit when he was wrong, to say "I don't know" when he didn't know and to apologize to those falsely accused, just as if they were grown-up people.

Don't think it was all one-sided. He taught them something too. He taught them to look up "insubordinate" in the dictionary. He taught them a new method of subtraction which he invented on the spot. Most important he taught them that teachers can make mistakes just like any other person.

"Well," said the teacher across the hall. "How was the first day of teaching?"

"Fine," he answered. "They were a little fresh in the morning but I got them into shape by afternoon."

"Really?" she said. "That's odd. They are the nicest group of children I've ever seen."

"Well," said his principal. "How was the first day of teaching? You're lucky, that class is the best this school ever had."

"Yes," he answered. "They rounded into shape pretty well after they gave me a hectic morning."

"Well," said his wife. "How do you feel after your first day of teaching?"

"I've never been so tired in my life. Every bone and muscle aches. I didn't think I'd get through the day."

"How are the kids?"

"Swell. They're going to be the best class that school ever had just as soon as they round me into shape."

Democracy and
the Desperate Despot

*M*Y BOYHOOD dreams revolved around the Naval Academy at Annapolis. Those long lines of white caps, those arms swinging in unison gave me a real kick. I would often picture myself striding along at the head of the battalion with that fancy sword. Unfortunately my dreams of a naval career were stifled by a childish aversion to mathematics too deeply rooted to be overcome by the recommendation of even the most sympathetic of congressmen. Then came World War II and minor handicaps involving square root were overlooked. I didn't get to carry a sword but I did learn to march and I liked it. And yet, outside of the esthetic value of nice straight lines and the disciplinary value of learning to do what you're told, I never gave any real significance to marching. Only when I began teaching did the "order from chaos" aspects of lining up become clear to me. Obviously my years of military training would now be put to use.

The educator, confronted daily with the logistic problems inherent in moving thirty squirming elementary school children from classroom to lunchroom, soon learns the value of military movement. A truly dedicated elementary teacher would do well to familiarize himself with Wellington's Peninsula Campaign, Na-

17

poleon's Hundred Days and Montgomery's masterful deployment at El Alamein.

The need for orderly movements may not be apparent to the uninitiated. After all, the children know the way out of the room. Why not just open the door and step aside? The result of such a drastic step might well be likened to a mass launching of three hundred guided missiles, each one containing a defective inertial guidance system. The children would ricochet from the walls, each other, and passing principals. The weak would perish, resulting in smaller classes but madder parents.

No, in order to evacuate the children, we must line them up.

The line-up in itself creates many problems. Alphabetical arrangement has the advantage of being quite permanent but results in much murmuring and unhappiness from the XYZ group. Reversed alphabetical order gives the XYZ's a big lift, but soon the ABC's are in a state of unrest. Working from the middle toward both ends creates confusion unless you can say the alphabet backward from L. Besides, all the world of children is divided into two parts: those who want to be first, and those who want to be last.

To most, being first seems to be a prestige item, somewhat akin to owning the only swimming pool on the street. America would not be America without equality of opportunity and it is obvious, to paraphrase Orwell, that the opportunity of those nearest the door is more equal than others. A good counterbalance here is to rotate the seating arrangement giving everyone a fair shot at the Number One spot.

Last place is even more of a problem. If everyone is trying to win, to come in last is easy. On the other hand if you have four all trying to lose, you're in trouble. The answer to this stickler is to move about the room beating them into line with the flat of your yardstick.

Then there's the problem of segregation of the sexes. No red-blooded fourth, fifth, or sixth grade boy would be caught dead standing near a girl. Misogyny to this age group is a way of life. (Sometime, however, a precocious sixth-grader may surprise you.)

So, we solve the problem of name-calling and at the same time

18

put in a plug for good manners by lining them up in two lines and letting the ladies go first.

Now they're lined up and moving out but you find yourself in another quandry. Shall you, the teacher, lead the line or bring up the rear? Let's look carefully at the aspects of this question.

The line leader is the pace setter, and as any good teacher knows, pace is an important factor in orderly movements. If the pace is too fast gaps appear, people begin running to catch up, and soon, sparked by the fear of being left behind, the whole herd is in full stampede. On the other hand, if the pace be too slow, someone will shove, step on heels, or trip. This results in a series of isolated fist fights very difficult to quell. "Well," you say. "This being the case the teacher should lead and be the pace setter." This shows little forethought on your part.

You've forgotten that, in the interest of rebuilding chivalry, we've put the boys last. Boys, some with baseball bats, are not to be trusted out of your sight. One solution is to scurry back and forth like a chipmunk preparing for winter.

A good compromise is to select a short-legged girl to lead and give her strict instruction as to stopping places. This is important since once out of sight around a corner the pace will automatically increase. A well-trained leader will wait for the go-ahead at every door and every corner. Perhaps you'll have a few protests from PTA stalwarts who decry militarism and murmur about neo-Nazi youth groups, but stick to your guns.

A few other things bear mentioning in this area. One child who will plague you continually is the nonconformist. This lad or lass just cannot stay in line. Some may even look upon them as defiant children baiting their teacher. I feel this to be an oversimplification. The trouble here is more deep-seated. Inner ear trouble perhaps, or an aversion to the backs of other people's heads. Try to reason with the child, and if that doesn't work, tap him behind the ear with the butt end of your swagger stick.

One teacher trap into which countless members of the profession have fallen is the unequivocal command. "All right, class," you bellow. "Line up right here," pointing to a stop at your feet.

The mad rush that follows would frighten a Roxy usher. The first child immediately climbs onto your shoeshine and the rest jostle and shove into place. No sense stepping back since they'll just step forward. Forethought again. You must designate a spot. "Line up at the edge of the walk," or "Line up at the steps," gives indication of planning.

One last item revolving around "lining up" is what I call the Friend Problem. This usually occurs in the cafeteria line. A series of screams and protests brings the teacher. "He cut in, he cut, he cut in," choruses the group, pointing to the guilty one.

"Did you cut in?" you ask.

"No!" is the prompt reply. "Charlie let me get in in front of him. He's my best friend." The value of such friendship cannot be denied and it would be a darn shame to break it up so . . . Send them both back to the end.

Pupil gossip to the contrary, teachers are human and share human weaknesses, such as an inability to be in two places at once. In the supervision of six hundred children by twenty adults a need for delegation of authority will soon become apparent. In the army the first lieutenant is not expected to do the whole job himself but is given sergeants and corporals to assist him. The teaching profession came up with the same idea years ago. Just about every school has a group of children deputized to act in the name of the teacher. They are called by various names: Safety Patrol, Safeties, Junior Police, etc. The duty of a Junior Policeman is to supervise and safeguard his schoolmates.

Appointments to the force come by seniority (upper grades only), deportment (only the best-behaved), and achievement (no mark below a C). The result is as fine a body of public-spirited citizens as you will find anywhere.

Each is issued a belt, a badge, and in schools with affluent PTA's, a yellow rain hat and slicker; each is assigned a post; a captain and lieutenants are elected and the patrol is ready to go into action.

The teacher in charge of the Safety Patrol is usually young and enthusiastic. (That's because it's his first year of teaching. Anyone with more than one year's experience will take on the Safety Patrol job only under threat of immediate dismissal.) Being young and enthusiastic he will organize his patrolmen, instruct them in minute detail as to their responsibilities and privileges and, in fact, will leave no stone unturned in his search for an effective police force, feeling, wisely enough, that the success of this operation can but reflect glory on his organizational ability. I'll bet that if this man were placed in charge of the New York Police Department he would be a resounding success. Dealing with elementary school policemen is another matter.

Take the problem of physical force. The patrol has been called upon to enforce the rules of the school. On the first day they proudly trot their first case before our enthusiastic teacher. It's a second-grader and in order to prevent his escape they have each twisted an arm behind his back. The lad is in obvious pain, tears streaming down his face. After ascertaining the operative ability of the child's arms, the teacher begins hearing the case.

"What did he do?" he asks.

"He got out of line," comes the answer.

"He what?"

"He got out of line at the cafeteria. He dropped his ice cream money and went to get it."

"Well, that was all right."

"Gee, Mr. Hannan, you told us if anyone got out of line we should bring him to you."

Already on his very first day our young teacher has run into the problem of literal interpretation of his words. He assembles the entire patrol and explains that "out of line" means disorderly and the words "bring him to me" mean to escort the culprit, not physically drag him.

As the meeting ends, he feels sure the misunderstanding has been cleared up, but he will soon discover that these words will continually rise up to plague him. Countless charges of mistreatment of prisoners by the patrol will haunt him throughout the year.

He will also find his time pretty well taken up in the adjudication of the many violations observed by the patrol people. His head will whirl with the multitudinous transgressions of an obviously delinquent school population: Running in the halls. Fighting in the playground. Pushing in line. Talking in the auditorium or Taking stairs two at a time.

He will also find that not one of these cases is a clear-cut transgression. The patrolman makes the charges. The culprit denies all knowledge of the incident. Witnesses are called for both sides. A decision is made.

Picture this repeated ten times before class in the morning, twenty-five times during lunch, and twenty times after school and you'll see why eventually our young and no longer enthusiastic teacher will hit upon the idea of a court in which each case will be heard and judged by the violator's peers. He pictures himself sitting back, observing, giving wise counsel when needed, letting the children put democracy into action. This dreamy bubble is soon pricked when the judge begins to hand out sentences.

> Fighting in the playground—Stand with forehead and toes touching the wall five hours a day for a week. [Darn those horror movies.]
> Pushing in line—Stay after school for one hour for two months.
> Talking in the auditorium—Eat a bar of soap.
> Taking stairs two at a time—Bring both parents to school to accompany you as you climb the stairs one hundred times.

Our young but tired teacher feels that he must intervene here. He asks the court's permission to speak and after a long wait is reluctantly granted such permission. He then explains that in a democracy we make the punishment fit the crime. He asks the jury if they don't feel there is something wrong with the sentences of the court. After a long consultation, the foreman of the jury is ready with his answer.

"Yes, Mr. Hannan," he says. "We feel that the judge was too darned easy." Court is not adjourned but abandoned.

By mid-year our no longer young teacher has had an overdose of Safety Patrol. In order to preserve his sanity he develops a system for handling each case as it is brought before him. He appears to listen intently as the misdeeds of the culprit are outlined.

If the child is in third grade or below, he shakes a finger under its nose and warns, "Don't let this happen again."

If the child is above the third grade, he tells him he'll see him after school. Nothing ever happens after school but the child worries a lot.

Serious violations are sent to the principal. This admission of defeat is hard to take—but what is a tired, old teacher to do? Next September a new, young, enthusiastic teacher will show up with a brand-new table of organization.

"The platoon system is the answer," he explains. "Every platoon will have a patrol area and all violators are to be brought directly to me. If anyone gets out of line he'll answer to the court I'm going to set up."

Last year's leader starts to tell him about the words "brought" and "out of line." He thinks perhaps his own experience with the court system will help enlighten him. He starts to speak a warning but suddenly realizes that true leavening can come only from experience and he changes his mind.

"Gee," he says, "that sounds great. That court system is a real innovation. You know if you do a good job on this it will be a real feather in your hat." The tyro nods enthusiastically and goes back to work on the large chart of trouble areas.

"I'll tell you one thing," muses the defeated one. "If no young, enthusiastic teacher shows up next year and they stick me with the job again, I'm arming the entire patrol with short lengths of rubber hose. They say it never leaves a mark."

Some time early in his career a new teacher will become stifled by the multiplicity of duties which occupy time better used on correcting papers or checking the scratch sheet. He will hit upon the idea of class officers. A class president could take attendance, conduct opening exercises and maintain discipline while the teacher finishes his mid-morning coffee. A vice president will backstop his chief (it's always a problem finding chores for vice presidents).

The class treasurer can take over the nasty little duties such as collecting for the many worthy causes which arise during the school year (paying for windows broken in baseball games is just one such cause).

The class secretary also has quite an important job, at least the class secretary in my class does. One of her many duties is to see that each and every child has his daily supply of notices to take home. If this responsibility is placed on my shoulders, it is quite apt to be forgotten. The result is an invitation to the PTA meeting getting home two weeks after the meeting night. When my secretary handles notices, they go home daily in twos and threes and not ten or twelve every Friday as when I'm in charge.

In addition to these very valuable services the election of class officers gives the children a chance to take an active part in democratic procedures, thereby preparing them for life in these United States.

Left to their own devices the children soon discover how our elections work. They find that a vote has value, and unless checked, will vote for the highest bidder. They also find that votes for a friend can be rounded up by discreet distribution of bubble gum, threats of a physical nature, or logrolling.

Stuffing the ballot box is not unheard of in sixth grade. It would appear that political chicanery is an inherited trait. The teacher who discovers 53 votes have been cast for a candidate when the class population is only 32 need not be too shocked. Remember that, although lying and stealing are known to be evil even to first-graders, political dishonesty is accepted by a good segment of the adult world. But teachers in general are a naïve crowd—and after preaching the values of political integrity, he throws out the old election and calls for a reform government. The children, anxious to be honest and upright, will do as requested and vote for those they like best.

Now any practical politician will tell you it's great to vote for your friends but who says they will make good officers? Teachers, being as far removed from practical politics as anyone, are well pleased with the idea of friendship and loyalty playing a part in the campaign. Disillusionment will set in when they discover who has been elected to help govern the class.

President—The lad who has broken every class rule.

Vice-president—His best friend, the strongest boy in the room.

Secretary—A sweet little girl who can't write a coherent sentence.

Treasurer—A nice lad with lots of friends and this psychological thing about Arithmetic.

At this point a teacher prone to panic might be frightened into abandoning democracy as a way of life and begin to stump for a dictatorship. No need to despair, all you have to do is play the modern Machiavelli.

The first step is to dump the incumbents. A *coup d'état* is necessary and easily accomplished. The whole election is declared null and void because it took place on Thursday and everyone knows that Tuesday is Election Day in the United States. The teacher declares a new Election Day and goes to work on a list of qualifications for candidates designed to eliminate all but those he wants. In other words, he rigs the whole election.

Even after the election, the problems are not all solved. Children granted authority tend to become ultra-officious. This, combined with a natural, childlike ruthlessness, tends to create friction in the classroom.

Let's take a hypothetical case.

Doreen, heretofore a pillar of classroom society has violated one of the cardinal principles of the Class Constitution: she left her lunch box in the aisle.

If the teacher were dealing with this case he would merely point out the transgression, which would immediately be corrected. No such slipshod police work will be tolerated by the class officers. Doreen is found guilty and is given the usual sentence for such a violation. She has to write the class motto, "Safety is Nice," five hundred times. That night Doreen falls off her back porch and breaks her writing arm. Do her judges have mercy upon her? They certainly do. She is given an extra day to finish because she writes so slowly with her left hand. That's the way it is with kids.

I Hope He Doesn't Ask But I Betcha He Will

$\mathcal{A}$ LARGE part of the creative output of many young minds is devoted to perfecting excuses calculated to avoid work and the monotony of school. The most effective means of avoiding school-work is, of course, outright escape. Fairly consistent success is obtained by the statement, "I gotta see the nurse." This statement is made at least once a day to every teacher, in every elementary class-room in every school in the country lucky enough to have a school nurse.

It might well be that the child has a broken rib or a ruptured spleen. Then again it might be that the child has heard that the PTA will pay the taxi fare home for a sick youngster (the grin of a third-grader who has faked out the entire system of education and arrives home unexpectedly in a cab cannot be equaled). But it's more than likely that it's time for Social Studies period.

Every teacher is bound by conscience to listen to each complaint having to do with the health of a child. A child who seems sincerely concerned about his bodily ills will get to see the nurse; but the habitual malingerer has his day too. The gold-bricks have developed sincerity to a fine art. Two or three times a week this type will approach the desk, his face a mask of bravely borne pain. Usually there will be some outward sign, some manifestation of medical

29

crisis. Perhaps a dirty handkerchief around the wrist or an even dirtier bandage plastered across the back of the neck. Thinking to expose this fraud you may force removal of the bandage. Believe me, these kids have been checked out before. Under each bandage you will find a cut, burn, or mosquito bite, microscopic perhaps, but present. You have no choice but to send him to the nurse.

The constant traffic between classroom and nurse's office can be very trying. Right in the middle of your best pitch for the inversion method of fractional division a hand will go up. Glowing with your prowess as a teacher, eager to answer any and all questions, you call on the frantically waving paw. "Mr. Hannan," she calls, "kin I go to the nurse?" Several such incidents may lead you to consider drastic steps to control the hypochondriac.

The next time the child asks to go to the nurse you take a harsh attitude. "Listen, you're not really sick. Every other day at nine fifty-five you're up here asking to visit the nurse. You just sit right down and pay attention." The next morning you receive a nasty note from the girl's irate mother. Seems Susie had a temperature of 102.8 and was in the early stages of mumps.

Shaken by this incident you become a fall guy for any hare-brained story that the "chronics" give you. In fact you become so soft that the nurse, usually an easygoing type, begins to give you hard looks when she passes your door. Obviously you must select a middle course. You must become a competent judge of human nature, a keen-eyed diagnostician, and above all a cynic whose sympathetic attitude matches that of a Marine Corps drill instructor.

The Habitual Nurse-Seekers have a few outward signs which make them comparatively easy to spot:

1. Consistency. They ask each and every day and are not discouraged by refusal.

2. Punctuality. Each has a certain subject they'd like to miss. If that subject is taught at 9:45 every day, that's the time illness strikes.

3. Frequency. If refused at their regular hour they ask several times through the day and if told to wait 15 minutes to see if they

30

feel better, appear at your desk exactly 14½ minutes later stating that they feel worse than ever.

4. A pained expression. This is usually accompanied by convulsive clutching of the afflicted area.

Discouraging the seeker-after-health can be an outsized job for an inexperienced teacher. If you do as I did and adamantly refuse to allow anyone to see the nurse you may bring down parental wrath, or worse, may have to send posthaste for hot water, disinfectant, and the janitor. This super-tough attitude solves nothing. A true malingerer cannot be discouraged by a mere teacher. On the other hand, those who are really ill will not be helped by threats.

My Compromise Plan works fairly well. I know the child is faking, the child knows I know, so we have an unwritten pact. Every fourth time the child asks to see the nurse, I let him. In between the answer is no. In this way each of us has the satisfaction of winning and learns to accept loss in a gracious manner.

For example:

Monday, 9:10 A.M.—Arithmetic assignment, page 110. Marie approaches the desk. "Mr. Hannan," she whispers, "I can't see out of my left eye." (By sixth grade they have discovered that better results are obtained if the symptoms are dramatic.)

"Well, Marie," answers the old pro, "use just the right until nine-thirty and then see me again." Nine-thirty comes and goes but Marie finding page 110 fairly easy has a marvelous restoration of vision.

Tuesday, 10:15.—The teacher asks for last night's homework. Marie advances to the desk moaning in pain. "Mr. Hannan," she croaks, "I gotta see the nurse. I think my right ear is frostbitten."

Mr. Hannan speaks not but leads Marie over to the window and points to the thermometer on the windowsill. Marie nods knowingly, they exchange conspiratorial smiles and she returns to her seat to think up a good excuse for not having her homework.

Wednesday, 11:15—Marie, bored with dull routine, advances clutching her side. "Mr. Hannan, I gotta see the nurse."

"What's the trouble, Marie?"

"It's my 'penndix. I had a lotta trouble with it last year in Miss Smith's class."

"I know just how you feel, Marie. I have the same trouble myself." From then till 11:30 (lunch) you happily exchange symptoms.

Thursday, 10:02—Marie limps painfully up to the desk. "Mr. Hannan, I think my leg is broke."

Mr. Hannan throws in the towel. "Better go down and have it set, Marie. I'll give you ten minutes."

"Sure, Mr. Hannan," she yells cheerfully. "I won't be long." She limps gracefully from the room. In about six minutes she's back scowling. "The nurse is out. The principal says I should bathe it in Epsin Sauls, whatever that is." She slumps dejectedly into her seat, her day ruined.

Friday, 9:25—A note from the nurse.

Dear Mr. Hannan,
    Haven't seen Marie all week. Is she ill?

                                        Signed,
                                        Worried

Next to escape the best method of whiling away the hours between 9:00 and 3:00, known by all children to be the deadliest part of the school day, is to bring in something to play with, some toy or puzzle. By June any teacher worth his or her salt should have the right-hand drawer of the desk filled with an admirable collection of such objects.

A scientific study made by a prominent educator (me) has shown that the number of playthings brought to school by a sixth-grader is in direct ratio to his Arithmetic mark. A "D" student will usually have two or three items taken from him each week while the child who is carrying straight "A's" will bring perhaps one or two a year (usually a lightning calculator or a pocket slide rule).

Like the man who doesn't like to wear torn underwear because he might get into an accident and end up in the hospital, I sometimes find myself worrying about that bottom right-hand drawer of my desk. Suppose a school board member on a routine inspection happened to glance into my desk? My principal or the superintendent

32

I wouldn't mind. They, having been teachers themselves, would understand, but, a member of the Board of Education! What would they think of a teacher who in his desk drawer kept:

1. Three complete sets of baseball cards (including Ted Williams who you might not know has a separate gum card contract and is quite hard to get).

2. A set of three wax fangs (designed to frighten your buddies).

3. Two decks of cards (one marked).

4. A punchboard (first prize—a bottle of bonded bourbon).

5. A bottle of ink (green).

6. A bottle of ink (red).

7. A bottle of ink (mixed).

8. Nine water pistols (an aquatic rumble nipped in the bud).

9. Eight combs (at sixth grade a girl begins to worry about her appearance).

10. A bag of marbles (60 puries).

11. A dog collar (the dog escaped during Spelling).

12. A muskrat trap (it was jammed open and caused me many a touchy moment while filing it).

13. Twenty-six comic books (only two educational comics, *Moby Dick* and *The Wealth of Nations*).

14. A wide assortment of plastic objects. Some are recognizable but most appear to be the tops of things or the bottoms of things.

15. Forty-seven ball-point pens all of which have advertising messages printed on the barrel (that constant clicking drives me mad).

16. A shot glass. (?)

17. Four pair of dice and a small roulette wheel (I did have a sporty group that year).

This of course is but a partial listing, a more detailed enumeration would take a far thicker tome than this.

A more basic problem and one which may seem troublesome is the question of the legality of this confiscation. Let me put your minds at ease. It is practically unknown for a child to go home and tell his parents that, "Mr. Hannan took my bullets," since such a statement would inevitably be followed by the question, "What in

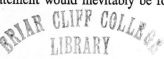

33

the name of Samuel Colt were you doing with bullets in school?" Rather than place himself in such a precarious situation the child will remain mum.

A more pressing problem, at least toward the end of June, is what will you do with that drawer full of junk? I've used several different techniques.

My first year of teaching I put them in a burlap bag and dropped it in the Passaic River. This resulted in an embarrassing incident in which the SPCA accused me of drowning kittens.

Another time I boxed the whole mess and sent it to a nearby boarding school. However, upon my return to school in September I found it on my desk along with a nasty note from the school's director. I thought my gesture a nice piece of professionalism, feeling that teachers in these private schools should be exposed to the hard, cold facts of public school education. Sort of in-service training. It certainly was a slap in the face to have my gift rejected.

Of course you might return each object to its proper owner. This though leads to difficulty. Some of the children might construe it as a sign of weakness. Besides, nobody remembers who contributed what to the pot.

It would seem that your best bet is burial. Again this must be done in a manner that won't arouse suspicion. Midnight on a moonless night would be ideal if it were not for the gossip such clandestine goings-on might inspire in your neighborhood. Broad daylight and a frank admission of your object is the safest approach to this problem. Of course, I don't worry about this problem, myself. I have four kids of my own. I split the loot among them just before school opens in September. Let *their* teachers worry about what to do with the year's bag.

The least effective but most widely used method of passing time during the dreary day is chewing gum. Although it does not present physical escape as in seeing the nurse or mental escape as with toys or games (unless you could class an occasional large bubble as a toy), it does bring relaxation. Too, it often triggers incidents with the teacher which are recreational in themselves besides wasting the time usually taken up by grammar.

It is a well-known fact among those conversant with the science

34

and art of education that the learning process cannot go forward while the teachee is chewing gum.

A complete experimental study proving this theory was made in the early thirties by a young professor at a Midwestern university. Unfortunately this study was never published due to the untimely death of the professor's uncle. This uncle left his nephew an entire chicle plantation in South America. In order to properly manage this plantation the professor had to abandon his well-paying job and move South. He took the gum study with him in order to complete his final tabulation. However, in a one-in-a-million accident the entire study was lost.

The professor while barbecuing a suckling pig over an open fire was using the brief case containing the figures to fan the flames. Tragically the brief case slipped from his greasy fingers and flew into the fire. A heroic Indian lad started to reach into the inferno to rescue the smoldering object but the quick-thinking professor, ever mindful of the health of his employees, caught him by the arm, swung him around and rapped him a shot in the mouth. Then with a sad but courageous smile he watched his years of work vanish.

Never one to be daunted by adversity, the professor plunged into the management of his little holding, and despite his meager knowledge of the chicle industry, made an astounding success. Yet he remains humble and every year on his way to a three-month's sojourn at a Nevada health resort, stops to visit his old university and gives patronizing advice to those of his colleagues who care to listen.

Despite this catastrophic loss of the gum-chewing study, teachers everywhere know by instinct alone that the chewing of gum must not be tolerated in the classroom.

Gum chewing, in and of itself is entirely innocent. It is only when the chewing becomes a symbol of rebellion against constituted authority that the challenge must be met by the teacher. He begins by stating, clearly and strongly, early in the year, that gum chewing during classtime will not be condoned and anyone caught chewing will be dealt with most severely.

"Most severely" is a blanket threat which means the teacher has no idea what punishment to administer but will think of something when the occasion arises. The occasion arises the next day.

The culprits, eight in number, are marched to the front of the room, made to deposit the gum in the wastebasket, and are given a strong lecture on obedience to the rules of the school. As any schoolboy knows the deterrent effect of a strong lecture is negligible, and the next day at least six of the eight will be back. It's time for an Example, sometimes called Horrible.

In this case each chewer is required to copy, word for word, everything in the encyclopedia beginning with gum. This includes: Gum, chewing; Gum Arabic; Gum Resins and Gumbo (see Okra). This exercise is guaranteed to discourage gum chewing among the easily discouraged but don't believe for a minute that such action will bring chewing to a complete halt in the classroom. The chewers will simply move underground.

The surreptitious chewer can be a nagging annoyance to any teacher. In the first place they are extremely hard to detect. Through long practice they are able to chew with barely moving jaws. In the second place, they have a variety of tricks. One stratagem the gum chewers have perfected is the Diversionary Move. Children are selected to act as the diverters. Their job is simple. They are to chew vigorously on their tongues, taking no pains to conceal jaw motion. The greenhorn teacher, aghast at such temerity, will inevitably fall into the trap. "Edward," she will scream, "spit out that gum!"

A slow smile of triumph spreads over Edward's face. "I ain't chewing gum, ma'am," he states.

"Well then," she asks in her innocence, "what are you chewing?"

"My tongue, ma'am," answers Edward and amid gales of laughter from those who were primed for the joke opens his mouth for inspection. Not a pretty sight!

This retort is most baffling since no one has ever forbidden tongue chewing, only gum chewing. Even the most sympathetic student will spot, "Well, you better stop" as the weakest of weak statements in this case.

If this conspiracy works well, the teacher will be trapped in this fashion four or five times by the end of the day. Needless to say, discipline has been undercut and gum chewing spreads since the teacher can no longer be sure who is guilty of an infraction.

The wise teacher need not despair. There is a solution to this seemingly hopeless situation. Instead of making a positive statement such as, "Get rid of that gum," ask a question, "Are you chewing, Edward?"

If he has been trying to trap you, you've spiked his guns since all he can say is, "No." If, on the other hand, he IS chewing, he can take one of two courses: he can tell the truth and take his punishment, or he can swallow the gum.

This second method is easily spotted by the convulsive movement of the throat which accompanies the ingestion of a large wad of gum. This method can be discouraged by a vivid, if lying, description of the havoc caused to the digestive system by such an insoluble lump.

A skilled teacher should have no trouble keeping gum chewing at the minimal level. However, complete elimination of the problem is impossible and this fact should be faced early in life and lived with without rancor.

For some children gum chewing in defiance of authority is a way of life, and any punishment which accrues to them in this regard is looked upon as a sort of martyrdom. Through it they gain stature in the eyes of their contemporaries and well-concealed respect from their teachers. You've just got to admire a kid who's written the entire section on gum fourteen times in three months.

American chewing gum is famous throughout the world due to the untiring jaw movements of the masticating GI of World War II. Our propensity for gum chewing has received international recognition, even notoriety. This ability is not come by in any haphazard fashion. We learn it in school.

The most ingenious and exasperating excuses concocted by the younger generation revolve around homework. The value of homework is doubted by many educators but parents expect it, teachers give it, and so the only honorable thing for the student to do is try to avoid it.

Some teachers, the really hard-hearted ones, will accept no excuse for a missed homework assignment. To me a masterly excuse, obviously concocted with some thought, is a challenge. A warm glow steals over me as I attempt to match wits with a past master of such evasions. Just listen to them:

1. "I forgot my book in school."

This is tricky. Maybe he did forget his book. How to ascertain whether or not he took his book home last night would baffle Holmes himself. Some favor the "jelly sandwich clue." This consists of checking the book for sticky pages. If last night's assignment has a smeared edge you can be sure he looked, found himself wanting, and decided to lie about the whole thing.

However, since I've had boys who could jelly up every page in the book just putting on a cover, this method may lead to wrong-conclusion-jumping, a disease well calculated to keep a teacher in hot water.

My recommendation here is to be completely unreasonable. Assign the entire section on education in the Encyclopaedia Britannica to be copied word for word. This will result in one of two reactions. Either the lad will break down and cry (in which case he really did forget the book) or else he'll shrug. If the latter occurs you'll know he's guilty of deliberate malingering but you'd better just forget the whole incident. Anyone who shrugs after an assignment like that has no intention of doing it anyway.

2. "I left my homework home."

This is easily proved. At lunchtime you stand at the door of the school watch in hand. You allow just enough time for the round trip home and back. The honest but careless will appear sweaty but smiling, homework in hand. Others will have excuses of great originality:

a. "The door was locked and my mother was out."

b. "My mother's sick."

c. "My grandmother's deef and she didn't hear me knock."

Obviously such a list is endless. Again I must recommend the Britannica gambit, unless truth serum is readily available.

3. "My little brother scribbled all over it and I had to throw it away."

"You could have brought it in and showed me you had completed the assignment."

"But, Mr. Hannan," is the innocent reply, "you said if it ain't done neatly don't bother bringin' it." You've lost this round, may as well be as graceful as possible in defeat.

4. "The dog ate it." This is a beauty. Truth shines from this lad's eyes. The smile on his lips denotes an inner serenity that could only come from complete belief in his own words. Don't doubt for a minute the dog ate the paper. You may strongly suspect that it was first smothered with gravy or chopped up with the horsemeat but the story as stated is true. Why would a boy deliberately feed his homework to the dog? That's simple. He just wants to be able to truthfully state in a loud voice, "The dog ate it." The boy is a ham and will do anything for a laugh. You can't prove a thing.

5. "The baby ate it." See number 4 above, ignoring the sentence about gravy. Babies will eat anything—raw.

6. "I had to go to a Scout meeting." The motto here is "Be Prepared." Check with the Scoutmaster beforehand as to time and length of the meeting. I guarantee it will not interfere with homework, all Tenderfeet protests to the contrary.

7. "It rained last night." This is what's known in the trade as a "stopper." What in the name of progressive education does that have to do with not doing homework? Here you must attempt to analyze the devious workings of a child's mind.

a. "It was raining when I got out of school. If I had taken my book home it would have gotten wet. After what you told us about our fathers paying for these expensive books by their taxes I thought you wouldn't want me to ruin it by carrying it in the rain."

b. "It was raining at homework time and I hoped it would rain all night so I could use the 'expensive' book excuse and leave my book at home."

c. "I live in a flood area and we sat up all night waiting to see if we had to put the TV on top of the piano."

d. "My grandmother lives with us and she says electricity attracts lightning so we had to sit in the dark till bedtime."

8. "I rode my bike to school." This is the deluxe stopper or

39

"stunned teacher" excuse. It seems that if you ride your bike to school, and you don't have a bicycle basket, you can't carry books because it's dangerous riding with one hand; therefore you leave your books in school and have a ready excuse for no homework. Any teacher who has been confronted with this excuse is well aware that no adequate response or punishment is possible. This child is obviously gifted and should be immediately referred to the school psychologist for placement in the Exceptional Child Program. It might be well to enclose a covering letter, warning about the boy's keen insight into the workings of a teacher's mind.

How to Teach Things You Don't Know

$\mathcal{I}$N RECENT years there has been a widespread rumor that "they don't teach the way they used to." Coupled with it is the feeling that we spend "too much time on frills." The reasoning behind these two attitudes is easily explained. Twenty years ago we had Reading, Writing, Arithmetic (sometimes called the three R's by those who have never mastered the intricacies of Spelling), History, Geography, and Spelling, and everyone went home for an hour's lunch break. Children hated school.

Today most kids like to come to school. This kind of attitude is in direct contradiction to our puritanical heritage which is, "If you like it, it can't be any good." Children like school because today's schools have jazzed up the curriculum by the addition of some pleasantly profitable subjects such as Physical Education, Music, and Science.

It's the teachers that hate school now and for good reason. No longer are they secure in their command of subject matter. Let's take Physical Education.

They used to call it recess and it was a wild fifteen minutes of screaming, running, pushing, shoving, and punch ball. Now it's called Physical Education and it's a class in which children are taught "large and small muscle control," "hand eye co-ordination," and "lead-up skills to major sports."

Some school districts are rich enough to hire physical education specialists even for the elementary grades but most elementary schools stumble along on the theory that a good teacher can teach anything, even the rudiments of downfield blocking. Under this mantle of omniscience we find three groups huddled.

Group I takes its job seriously and buys books on softball, soccer, and hand polo. This type is seen sweating in the sun giving batting instruction or ineptly demonstrating proper form in punting. Indoors it can be recognized by a painful limp caused by a pulled groin muscle.

Group II leans more toward the vocal and away from the physical. From its perch on an overturned wastebasket, it gives detailed instructions on how to carry out the activity. It often threatens to take off its sunglasses and demonstrate but has never been known to carry out this threat.

Group III is somewhat clannish. Two of them arrange to have their Phys. Ed. period together and, while the children cavort happily, three to a swing, or ski jump from the slide, the teachers chat seriously about the shocking neglect of children by parents.

Physical education as taught by the classroom teacher should have two aspects: Calisthenics and Sports. Calisthenics are good for muscle tone, teach co-ordinated movement, and give the children a warm-up for more strenuous activity. At least a portion of the Phys. Ed. period should be devoted to such exercise. The fact that the teacher is dressed in a suit and starched collar and looks like a damn fool doing deep knee bends, may have something to do with the widespread neglect of this healthful activity.

Most Phys. Ed. classes in the elementary school are conducted outdoors unless weather prevents. A visit to any school gymnasium anywhere in the country will immediately tell you why. Noise level can be likened to the test area of a jet factory. Smell, unmasked by deodorant, is overwhelming. Only a professional Phys. Ed. instructor is inured to these hardships. When inclement weather pre-

44

vents outdoor exercise the wise teacher prepares some classroom games in order to allow relaxation.

(If the inclement weather persists for, say a week, perhaps you better resort to a daily art period to shorten the long afternoon. If it lasts for a month you'd better use my system—I turn all hands to scrubbing decks and bulkheads and polishing brightwork. There'll be no idle hands to make devil's work on my tight little ship.)

One very upsetting feature of the Phys. Ed. program is that having to do with personal injury. Inevitably, someone in your class will be injured. Dealing with these injuries can be a harrowing experience unless you take a calm, fatalistic view. You must be like a surgeon with no emotional involvements permitted.

A few simple rules will help attain this objectivity. First remain calm at all times. Panic in your voice will lead to hysteria in an injured child. Check for blood. Without blood what injury can be serious—unless you want to mention that most rare occurrence, a concussion of the brain. If there is blood first aid is necessary so . . . send the victim to the nurse or the principal.

In handling the injured differentiate sharply between boys and girls as befits their respective roles in society. Boys who are hit with flung bats or laid low with illegal flying blocks are told to "rub it out, rub hard" or "walk it off and for God's sake stop crying."

Girls, on the other hand are assisted to the nurse's office by two close friends. No matter how minor the injury two sympathetic friends are necessary. Is it any wonder women live longer than men?

Unfortunately (for the teacher) the Physical Education program is not confined to a half hour each day. At least once a year a program of outdoor activities is planned. In my section of the country this quaint custom is called Field Day. How widespread the idea is I don't know but I'm sure if it is held at all it must follow this pattern.

Field Day consists of a group of athletic endeavors modeled roughly on Olympic track events. I say roughly because it is a rare Olympiad that shows us a potato race, a sack race, or a three-legged race.

45

The chairman of the whole picture is usually the male staff member with the most hair and the smallest belly, the theory being that youth is what's needed here. His job as over-all director is to obtain volunteers to supervise and score for the individual events. He tries the volunteer angle for a while but is finally forced to squeal to the principal who will then appoint the necessary volunteers.

The chairman plans the number of events, the methods of scoring, and the manner in which each is to be conducted. At a staff meeting, attended by the dragooned and sullen volunteers, he explains the whole idea. After several repetitions, none of which seem to have gotten his points across, he adjourns the meeting and reworks the whole plan. This second plan, though much simpler, is also about to be rejected when the principal, at the invitation of the chairman, puts in an appearance. Justice carries the day.

The chairman can hope for two kinds of weather on the appointed day. He can pray for torrential rain in which case the whole thing is off; or he can pray for a clear, sunny beautiful day, a day to put every one in good spirits. What he probably will get is a day that is alternately threatening and clear, one that will keep him a nervous wreck trying to decide on postponement.

Mind made up, he begins to lime the field. This means marking off the event areas with lines of lime. In no time at all the job is finished and the chairman is in to the nurse having his eyes washed out with a weak solution of boric acid.

Promptly at nine the festivities start. A runner enters the school grounds bearing a flaming torch. He streaks through the assembled multitude and plunges his torch into the pile of paper in the incinerator and the games are officially opened. (For those not too concerned with the dramatic the above may be eliminated.)

Each teacher marches her children to the designated area and the events begin. Such excitement—children milling about, cheering on their classmates, running for drinks of water, asking to go to the bathroom. And there in the center of the field is the chairman, megaphone in hand, shouting orders, co-ordinating activities, screaming at the stupid teachers who still don't understand the scoring.

46

By 9:15 it's raining. All enter the auditorium and begin to sing rounds under the direction of the chairman. He only knows two songs, "Three Blind Mice" and "Jingle Bells," so everyone is relieved when the sun comes out and they can return to the games.

But the day finally ends, the children go home, and he is free— free to total up the scores, for tomorrow the children will want their awards. Free to snap back at the teachers who blame him for the whole mess. Free to put cream on his face which managed to get sunburned even through the clouds. Free to try and knead that infernal cramp out of his left thigh. Free to call himself a damn fool for trying to broad-jump further than that big kid in sixth grade.

A day like this sure points up the need for physical fitness— especially among teachers.

In teaching Physical Education, there is one other tension-producing circumstance which I should mention here. Throughout our land there are well-meaning, dedicated groups called Little League managers, Little League coaches, Little League Boosters, and Little League auxiliaries. All have but one aim—the preservation of our national pastime.

Almost any parent who has a son in school can tell you about Little League. They can discuss team standings, the shortcomings of the coaches, the advisability of using the hit-and-run play when the runner is wearing his older brother's sneakers, and whose car is being used for transportation tonight. They might mention the fine, healthy, competitive American spirit engendered by the movement. If they do, you can be sure their son's team is in first place and he went 4 for 5 last night. Or perhaps they might mention the psychological harm, the traumatic experience boys of this age might undergo because of failure on the diamond. In this case their son's team is in last place and the only hit he's had was a hit on the head from a pop to short center.

When I was a young boy, there were serious, head-shaking discussions concerning the imminent demise of baseball. Softball was the coming thing, and hardball addicts were afraid that with so much emphasis on softball no one would ever learn to play baseball. I even began to worry a little myself. Not that I played baseball, I just worried a lot.

The worriers of yesteryear must be the satisfied oldsters of today when they glance around them and see every sand lot replete with backstop and grandstands and bulging with fully uniformed (if haphazardly fitted) youngsters sporting gloves that Dizzy Dean could never have possessed.

In fact the only thing missing is the fun. Everyone is deadly serious and black murmurs run through the stands if the umpire pulls a rock. (It should be noted that the umpire too is fully uniformed and squats behind the catcher in an air-filled chest protector. In bygone days some passing stranger would stand behind the pitcher and keep track of balls and strikes with a handful of pebbles.) A boy caught smiling doesn't have his heart in the game and is summarily benched.

What has this to do with education, you say? Well, eventually the lessons learned on the playing fields of suburbia filter back to the school.

Through the fall and winter the elementary school Physical Education program runs along quite smoothly. In the spring we move into softball and with great enthusiasm the boys trot out to play the first game (I never bother with practice—practice is boring). All but the two boys lounging against the fence. The teacher approaches them smiling. "What's the matter, boys, don't like softball?"

"We can't play."

"Oh, don't worry about that. I'll help you out if you don't know what to do."

"We know how to play but we can't."

"Why can't you?"

"Lefty won't let us."

"Lefty won't let you? Who's Lefty?"

"He's our coach and he says softball ruins your timing." Since these lads are fast approaching age twelve, development of timing is most important.

48

The teacher sets a trap. "What's timing?"

The boys exchange uncomfortable glances and shuffle their feet nervously. Finally the bravest speaks up. "We don't know what it is but Lefty says softball ruins it."

The teacher laughs lightly. "Suit yourselves, boys." He moves away, confident that a couple of days of watching the other boys having fun will bring them around.

The next day there are six boys lounging against the fence. Upon inquiry they fill him in on the details. It seems "Righty" told them throwing a softball would "roon" their arms.

On the third day the only boys left to play softball are Sy, whose broken nose hasn't healed properly from last year's spring training, and Larry, who is frank enough to admit that he doesn't like base-ball 'cause the ball hurts when it hits him. Obviously something must be done. Our teacher decides to investigate the coaches who are undermining his class discipline and the entire Physical Education program of the school system. "All right, boys," he asks, "who is Lefty?"

"He's our coach," comes a chorus. "He almost had a contract with the Dodgers but he hurt his arm."

"He ain't our coach." This from another group.

"Who's your coach?" he asks.

"Righty. He almost had a contract with the Yanks only his father made him go to work in his gas station."

One lone voice pipes up. "I play for Ambie."

"Ambie?"

"Yeah. He can throw with either hand. He played for Cincinnati for two weeks but he didn't like the way the manager was running the team so he quit."

Now he knows his opposition. But what can he do about it? His first impulse is to stomp into the principal's office, call the superintendent of schools, and demand a showdown that will prove once and for all who runs the schools.

It is hoped that cooler heads will prevail. Any outright attack which appears to put the school in opposition to Little League will

49

inevitably bring down cries of Un-Americanism on the heads of the Board of Education and the superintendent. Also, the teacher will lose his job.

His best bet is an invitation to his rivals to visit the school. Then he explains that, as much as he admires baseball, unfortunately he is not qualified to teach the game. He explains about the cost of expensive protective equipment, the inadequacies of the present softball diamond, the lack of qualified officials. As almost-professionals, they will understand his deep concern for any makeshift approach to the national pastime. A few hours of such diplomatic discussion may well result in their releasing their boys from the solemn, sealed-in-the-blood promise never to play softball.

There is one other alternative. If the kids won't play softball make them jump rope with the girls. That should bring any eleven-year-old boy into line in a hurry.

Unfortunately your Little League problems won't end with the return to sanity of the protagonists. A few more things will develop. One lad who up till now has been a fair student (if somewhat spotty in homework completion) suddenly stops work altogether. Diplomatic questioning will bring out the inevitable.

"My father says I'm the best player in Little League and ball players don't need no education."

It is well to point out that most of today's players are college men, that baseball takes brains as well as brawn, that a ball player who refuses to learn how to figure his batting average will still have to be able to read in order to find out how he's doing.

To face the horrible truth it does seem that more ball players read comic books than read Plato, and grammar doesn't play a strong part in the lives of the pennant-winning managers I've seen interviewed. Maybe schoolwork will make out better after the Series.

Another sure-fire incident will occur about the second week in June. After six weeks of rehearsal the class play is ready for the boards. The cast is keyed to its highest pitch, the leading lady confident and beautiful, the leading man nonchalant and almost handsome. The nonchalance has you worried because he's been a bundle

50

of nerves since he was drafted for the part. On the Friday before the Big Monday your fears are proved to be well founded.

"I," he states calmly (almost defiantly), "won't be here Monday night."

You laugh hollowly since this can only be considered a joke. "Why not?" you gasp, suppressing a note of hysteria.

"I'm pitching Monday."

When the furor has died down, when the Superintendent of Schools has left the building and the president of the Little League has wended his way homeward, when it is at last been firmly established that your leading man will appear on Monday even if it means the whole pitching staff's rotation will be upset, then—then you sit back, relax, and silently thank the powers that be that there is no school during the summer to interfere with the development of future big-leaguers. At the rate they're turning them out we'll need six Major Leagues. And, if one of my boys did just happen to make the big time, I suppose I'd be right there, cheering and informing those around me that: "I started that boy in baseball. I had him in the sixth grade. That's where they begin to develop their timing, you know."

Art

Art is another subject with which the teacher must be prepared to cope. By taking a course and reading a book he soon familiarizes himself with the aims and objectives of an Art program. Art gives the children an opportunity to express themselves creatively, it can give an observant teacher insight into the psychological workings of the children's minds. It also gives them an outlet for aggressiveness and encourages the release of their inhibitions.

The fact that the teacher's own inhibitions have prevented him from ever attempting art has no bearing on the case. It is in the curriculum: teach it. Buoyed up by the fact that others before him have survived, the teacher embarks upon an Art program.

Choice of medium is very important. Shall it be crayon, water color, cut-and-paste collage, charcoal, chalk, or tempera? If he's sensible he'll be chicken and confine everyone to crayon. This may inhibit artistic expression but it will save cleaning costs which inevitably mount with the use of liquid paint.

Next the eternal question asked by the children.

"What should we draw?"

Here the wisdom of the college class comes to the fore. Well he knows how little they will benefit from a subject dictated by the teacher. The psychological value of the whole project is lost. He won't fall into *that* trap. "Just draw anything," he tells them.

They exchange blank stares for a few minutes and then, here and there, a child will begin work. The teacher leans back. After the projects are properly under way, he strolls about, quietly, not wishing to inhibit in any way.

Ah! Here's a boy drawing a ship! No doubt reflects his anxiety about embarking on the sea of life. Here's another boy, he's drawing a ship, too. And here's another and another. Inquiry leads to the answer. Twelve boys are drawing ships because they saw Ed (the first lad) draw a ship. Well, anyhow Ed must have some motive for drawing a ship. Perhaps a beloved relative lost at sea or some such dark reason. He calls him up with his drawing.

"Ed," he asks gently, "why did you draw a ship? Someone you know lost at sea?"

"No," says Ed, "I draw a ship all the time 'cause that's my best thing. Last year in Mrs. Murdle's room I drew 237 ships."

The girls tend toward houses and the pattern is the same. Someone had an inspiration and before you can say Toulouse-Lautrec everyone for miles around is drawing the same house.

Three boys still have blank papers and after fidgeting for a half hour waiting for their original creation the teacher finally asks, "Why aren't you fellows drawing something?"

"Can't think of anything."

"How about a ship or a house?" he ventures timidly not wishing to inhibit.

"Nah!" comes the reply. "We're sick of drawing ships and houses."

After a careful analysis of this first experience he finally reaches some sound psychological conclusions. Obviously you can't expect a child to express himself freely if you restrict him to one art medium. Next time he prepares more wisely.

A variety of material is laid out. Various sizes of paper, crayons, chalk, water color, tempera, clay, flour and water and strips of paper for papier-mâché.

This time the results are much more satisfying.

At the period's end he has: Three ships and four houses of clay, six ships and two houses in tempera, one ship and two houses in charcoal, and eight ships and four houses in crayon. Three boys did nothing because they couldn't think of anything to do. Originality still seems hard to corner.

The next Art period finds our teacher ready. Desks are pushed together. Each child is armed with a large brush and a giant piece of white paper. A wide variety of paint is placed in the center of each group. "Now," he states firmly, "everyone has to be original."

"What's original?"

"No ships, no houses, just wide sweeping motions with the brush. Paint what you feel."

"I feel like painting a ship," says Ed.

"No ships."

After a few minutes Ed moves away from the group.

"What's the matter, Ed?" the teacher asks. "Why aren't you drawing?"

"Can't think of anything," replies Ed.

The rest of the group is warming to its task. At first they try a few timid strokes, but as you encourage the wide sweep of the brush, the party begins to liven up. Soon the brushes are moving gracefully across the white paper, dipping into the vivid colors and soon, too, they begin to move across shirt fronts and down the backs of dresses. One group, feeling the shackles of inhibitions dropping from them begin painting each other's faces. The bell finds the class a happy, multicolored mess and if one repressed emotion remains it certainly isn't noticeable.

As he wearily begins to clean the floor the teacher feels sure that tomorrow will bring the results of this freedom of expression home to the classroom.

What it brings is threatening letters from eight parents who accuse him, among other things, of irresponsible lack of "discipline" and a bill from Ed's mother, who despite his role of innocent bystander, managed to ruin a new pair of slacks.

A middle course must be found.

The next Art period finds things much better organized. Each child has a brush and paper. Small tins of paint are on each desk. Each child has handed in a release signed by a parent absolving the teacher from all culpability in the event of destruction of clothing.

A subject is selected (the same one for everybody) and the work begins. Things run very smoothly; he moves about warning against spillage and the use of too much paint, adjusting newspapers on desks. A noticeable tension soon reigns. One by one the children cease painting, wash out brushes carefully and finish up in pencil. Except for one gallon of red paint dropped into the sink by a butter-fingered young lady who grew overly anxious at his cautionary shouts, no calamitous incidents took place.

It should be pointed out that the pictures of the pilgrims landing on Plymouth Rock did appear quite stiff.

Still, as the years go by you find yourself more at ease during the Art period. Oh, it's true that the muscles of your thighs ache from tension and you do get a throbbing headache whenever paint brushes appear, but now, in your experience you've learned to cope. You're well aware of your limitations in the Art field, so early in each year you select one particularly good artist to be head of the Art Committee. All questions asked about shading, perspective, and proportion are referred to the chairman. That's democracy in action.

Clean-up, which in your early years you did yourself is now a delegated responsibility. In every class there are several children who fight for the opportunity to wash brushes and clean sinks. When confronted by papier-mâché they arm themselves with putty knives and make short work of lumps of paste and paper no matter where found—except on the ceiling. Although the scaffold they constructed out of four desks and six chairs seemed quite secure, a precautionary word from the principal containing the phrase "immediate dismissal if any injuries result" caused you to turn the job over to the janitor. His kind of hate you just have to learn to live with.

One last note on Art. A high percentage of "art" completed by some classes turns out to be maps.

Maps are fun, and even if the countries are unrecognizable by shape, the names are clearly printed. Map making has another value. Maps are Social Studies work. If you use crayon to color the countries that's Art. Now we have correlation or "two birds with one stone," Art and Social Studies. See how easy this teaching racket is? Just like coming down in the Guggenheim Museum.

Music

Another one of the arts to which the teacher is expected to expose the student is music. I like music. I like to listen to it and join that group gathered around the piano singing "I've Been Working on the Railroad" and "My Wild Irish Rose." I'm a music lover.

What I'm not is a great musician, a Leonard Bernstein. Yet each and every school day I am expected to lead my class in a patriotic song; and occasionally (horrible thought that it is) I am called upon to lead the entire school gathered in assembly in the first verse of "The Star-Spangled Banner."

At the risk of appearing subversive I would say this about "The Star-Spangled Banner"—well, I'll just say that when I pick the patriotic song to be sung we sing the "Battle Hymn of the Republic." It has a nice rousing chorus.

This business of leading groups in song might appear simple on the surface but the uninitiated should beware of such light treatment of a serious matter. I'll have you know that I spent one hour and twenty minutes per week for sixteen consecutive weeks learning about Music in the Elementary School. It was one of the most enjoyable courses of my career, and I know the reason. The instructor realized the poverty of the material with which he was working and adjusted his methods to fit the group. We had a great time.

One outstanding drawback to teaching this group how to teach music was the fact that only three people out of thirty-five knew how to read the notes. We were, in fact, a perfect counterpart of the average elementary school class down to and including those few who are often referred to as "listeners"—the tone deaf.

Undeterred by the seemingly hopeless odds facing him, our instructor proceeded to teach us about music. Not to read music but about music and how to teach music when you can't sing, and how to lead a group in song. Listening for the story as told by music, drawing to music were two other aspects of the course. By the end of the semester we were champing at the bit, just couldn't wait to flex our new-found musical muscles on the kids.

It's different though. . . .

I mentioned before that I'm inhibited. I don't like to stand up before groups and sing, not even if the groups happen to be sixth-graders. Frankly, my attempts at leading my class in song are somewhat haphazard. As a matter of fact months pass without me even opening my mouth in song. But, lest you begin feeling sorrow for the musically deprived group under my command, I will here state that they have more than enough musical experience.

First of all they have the music teacher who appears weekly to lead us. Here is where I shine. You see, I'm a follower, not a leader, but give me a good leader and I'm one of the loudest followers in the business. So carried away do I become that I frequently completely overshadow my entire class and have to be shushed by the music teacher (this from the mouse who barely squeaks when appointed song leader of the assembly).

When I first discovered my inability to stand up before my class and sing I was mighty discouraged. But after a few days of brooding I began to think about that course in Music for the Elementary

56

School and soon took heart. "After all," I reasoned, "my class need not be deprived of musical experiences just because of my personality quirk. After all we can always fall back on drawing to music."

You know sometimes I wonder if those kids really hear those things in music. If they did and I didn't this whole business could be quite frightening. I was leafing through the various pictures when the school psychologist happened by. Pointing to one particularly flamboyant attempt he clucked softly, shaking his head. "Who did this?" he asked.

"I don't know," I replied.

"See if you can find out, will you?" he said. "This child is clearly in need of therapy." I'm glad I didn't have my name on it.

I have, since that day, handed over my entire Music program to the music teacher with one exception. I handle the records. This is the simplest of all Music activities. It consists of playing a record and having the children listen.

There are two methods in general use.

1. Play the record to see if the children can guess what story the music tells.

2. Tell the story and have the children attempt to fit it into the ascending, descending moods of the music.

Let's take the "Grand Canyon Suite," by Ferde Grofé.

"Who can tell what a suite is?" A mass of waving hands testify to the eagerness of the group. Pleased by this early response you call on the most eager.

"A suite," he states firmly, "is like candy."

A little disappointed, you start to call on the next waving hand but suddenly find they have all disappeared. A suite, it seems, means the same to all. Discouraged but courageous, you plunge on and play the record and wait for reaction. Sure enough, as the music swells, more and more children seem anxious to participate. One little girl can contain herself no longer. She bursts forth with the big news.

"Mr. Hannan," she breathlessly exclaims, "that's the music for Philip Morris cigarettes." And she's right, thereby revealing one of the music teacher's most prevalent pitfalls. Today's children have an exhaustive knowledge of classical and semiclassical music. They recognize countless pieces but connect them strangely. "Gee," they breathe as they listen to the "William Tell Overture," "The Lone Ranger."

"I know that," they claim, listening to "The Flight of the Bumble Bee."

"Really," you say. "Well, that's wonderful. Who wrote it?"

"I don't know that," they answer, "but it's that song they play in the cartoon where the bear tries to steal the honey and the bees all chase him and the hunter saves him and later on the hunter falls off the cliff and the bear catches him and then the music plays that one we had yesterday—you know . . ."

"You mean Brahm's 'Lullaby'?"

"Yeah, that's the one and they go to sleep in the hunter's tent. Gee, that's a keen cartoon."

Lately, I've revised my whole approach to the problem of teaching Music. I've delved into our community resource file and come up with a group of interested citizen musicians who come in weekly to play for my class. They seem to be available any time I need them, and except for a liking for beards and black sweaters, fit right into my daily plans. They gave me this black beret and the kids seem to dig the whole bit. "Way out" is the way my class describes them.

Science

In this day of rocketry, space travel, and electric toothbrushes I would indeed be remiss if I overlooked an area which has begun to concern us all—Science.

In our all-out effort to Beat Russia we've driven introductory science down into the elementary grade while at the same time driving many teachers off their ever-lovin' rockers. Perhaps I can best show you the scope of the problem by detailing my own experiences.

One day, having turned my class over to the patient little music teacher, I was on my way to the cafeteria to check on a defective coffee urn. As I passed the door of the kindergarten I heard my name.

"Oh, Mr. Hannan," called the teacher, "could you come here a minute, please?"

"Sure thing," I answered. "My class is at Music. What are we doing, finger-painting?" The class laughed condescendingly at my little joke.

"Heavens, no," said the teacher. "Mitzi is just about to explain the principles of buoyancy. Please have a seat." So, with a small worry beginning to gnaw in my brain, I watched Mitzi using a plastic model of the *Arizona* and a large fish bowl, demonstrate conclusively that Archimedes was right.

Fearing the worst and having a few minutes to spare I toured a few of the rooms asking leading questions of the teacher. "What are you studying in Science?" I asked. My worst fears were realized.

The first grade was immersed in Boyle's Law on the compressibility of gases. Second-graders were concerned with the workings of a hydrostatic well, whatever that is. The third grade, with deep interest, was duplicating Mendel's famous genetic experiment.

With fluttering heart I entered the fourth grade and looked around. No complicated apparatus, no Science Corner, no erudite bulletin boards. I breathed a little easier. I approached the teacher with a comradely laugh. "Well," I said, "I guess we don't do as much Science as the lower graders." She looked shocked and pointed to a formula she had just written on the blackboard.

"Mr. Hannan," she said, "we are just starting a new unit. Read that!"

"$E = IR$," I read.

"Do you know what that is?" she asked.

"Well no, I really don't," I admitted.

"I do," said a little girl in the rear. "That's Ohm's Law."

"Ohm's Law?"

"Yes, E equals voltage, I equals amperage, R equals resistance. It's quite basic." I was in big trouble.

When I was in high school, Science was reserved for the eggheads. Today, Science is liable to turn up anywhere in the elementary grades, except in my class.

Oh, I've heard about the Russians' plan and I am in perfect agreement with anything we can do to counteract that threat. It's just that I hadn't counted on having to teach Science. My trip through the school had brought home in vivid detail the threat as it applied to me. I had two choices.

Teach Science or get out.

To me Science is equivalent to experiments and experiment means a laboratory, a long white coat, and chemicals. From fuzzy thinking it's but a short step to borrowing your son's chemistry set and whipping up a nice batch of invisible ink or perhaps making something that smells like rotten eggs. These two stand-out triumphs I remembered from my own boyhood. I felt duty bound to share them with my class.

The day of the experiments dawned bright and fair. I arrived a few minutes early and set up my material on the "laboratory table" next to my desk. As the children straggled in, they grouped themselves around, commenting on the various test tubes and beakers, curious about the day's events. I was a little impatient myself, wanting to impress the children with my keen grasp of scientific principles. Feeling a little like Pasteur and wishing I *had* purchased that white lab coat, I began mixing the ingredients for the rotten egg smell, holding the test tube high and pouring carefully as I had often seen in the movies. I will say that my first public experiment was an unqualified success. The smell of rotten eggs permeated the room, the halls, and eventually the principal's office. Since a good administrator wants to be conversant with all phases of education even if it smells, my boss appeared almost immediately.

"Mr. Hannan, what is causing that horrible odor?"

"Just something I mixed up in this test tube."

"What did you mix? Is it dangerous? How long will the odor last? Is this a learning situation or just some tomfoolery?" I was just about to quote Mark Twain by saying I didn't know when Randolph, Row 2, Seat 3, spoke up.

60

"The odor is caused by union of two parts hydrogen with one part sulphur, better known as hydrogen sulphide. It is probably the foulest odor known to man and emanates from rotten eggs and decaying vegetation. Upon contact with this gas, which is present in minute quantities in the atmosphere, silver will tarnish."

The principal smiled appreciatively. "Well, Mr. Hannan, you seem to be doing a bang-up job here. Science is what we need this day and age. Carry on with your work but please—close your door during experiments."

I avoided Randolph's eyes and started the invisible writing experiment. "You see, children," I began, "I'll write my name with this clear liquid . . ."

"Acetic acid," interrupted Randolph.

"It is not," I answered promptly. "It's vinegar."

"Vinegar *is* acetic acid," retorted Randolph.

"Who sez?"

"Vinegar is a deluted impure form of acetic acid produced by fermentation." This sounded like a direct quote so I took the coward's way out. I feigned deafness and went on with my experiment.

"Watch as I pass it over this candle . . ."

"You'd better light it first," said Randolph.

I sent Randolph to get matches from the janitor. As soon as he left the room I discovered some matches, lit the candle, passed the paper back and forth across the flame and was gratified to see my name clearly outlined on the paper. Before Randolph could get back I had cleared away my experiments and was ready to plunge into the day's Spelling. Before I could open my mouth Lee asked THE question, the one someone always asks. "Mr. Hannan," she said, "how does that work?"

"We'll discuss it tomorrow, Lee. Right now we're running a little late so . . . first word . . ."

"I can explain it in just a few words if you'll allow me," said Randolph slipping into his seat.

"Could you, Randolph?" breathed Lee enraptured.

"Sure," said Randolph and ignoring me completely explained

the whole thing. "Although I wasn't in the room [here he looked pointedly at me] I'm sure Mr. Hannan repeated the classic method of showing the chemical change which takes place when paper is coated with acetic acid."

"Vinegar," I muttered.

"This change caused the kindling temperature of that section to be lowered so of course when the paper is held over the flame the name chars first. Quite simple, really."

Randolph, who up to now had been a likable little lad, good in his studies and playing a right fair shortstop on the softball team, now became a thorn in my side. I tried to lose him. I went from geology to biology, from astronomy to paleontology, but no matter how I twisted and turned Randolph was right behind, or rather two or three steps ahead. He was quick to help by pointing out my many mistakes. When my experiments failed, which was almost always, he'd pick up the pieces and show the class just where I had gone awry. I was perpetually heavy-eyed and weary from the constant study necessary for even minimal success in my daily battle with Randolph.

I was just about to elect the second of my two possibilities and get out of teaching when I struck on my system. It is called the Hannan Plan for Expediting the Elementary School Science Program and although it is protected by an ironclad patent I hereby grant permission for its use to those who find Science teaching difficult.

Stripped to its bare bones the plan is quite simple. Select a committee made up of all those who like Science, chair it up with a Randolph, and turn the entire Science program over to the children. This resembles my solution to the Art problem, in that it is in line with democratic procedures, modern methods of education, and gets you out of a nasty hole.

Of course, the key to its success is the selection of a chairman with the vast store of knowledge necessary for such a project. This may seem a frightening task but you need not worry. It is a statistically proven fact that out of any group of twenty-five or more children, randomly selected, you will find at least three Science nuts, any one of whom will be able to carry the ball for you.

The biggest problem is finding these people and it is here that the neophyte is most apt to err. Beginning users of the Hannan Plan tend to follow the mistaken methods used in other, less scientific plans.

In line with these outmoded means of selection, they will first look for build, the feeling being that the skinnier the child the better the scientist. Next they will check eyes, glasses being mistakenly identified as the mark of the scientific brain. Last but far from least, the novice will check athletic ability. Any kid who can catch a ball is immediately eliminated, the theory being that physical co-ordination and scientific ability are contrary gifts and never occur in one body.

With such benighted thinking so prevalent in our land, it's a blessing we're not running *third* in the race to the moon.

The Hannan Plan for Expediting, etc., eliminates all such haphazard methods of selection. Based on a scientific principle first discovered by Learner the Learned back in 1242 and made practical by my modest self just four years ago, it bodes fair to being the prime means of selecting passees to whom the non-scientific Science teacher can pass the buck.

I call it the Ennui Syndrome. It is best discovered during some particularly dull subject, perhaps Grammar. When the group is sufficiently deep in the study of direct and indirect quotations, the teacher catfoots stealthily around the room observing the children in action. Some will be drawing pictures on the backs of their hands, others will be scratching their names in the desk tops, a few may be studying direct and indirect quotations, but the vast majority will be reading under cover of their large Grammar books. It is this group with which the Hannan Plan, etc., deals.

Some will be reading comic books, some sport encyclopedias (pocket size), and some Nancy Drew, but a few, the *precious few,* will be reading books with titles such as: *Rolicking with Rocks,* A Sixth-Grader Looks at the Uranium Problem; *Exothermic Action,*

Fun with Fire in Grade Five; $E = mc^2$, Einstein for the Pre-adolescent.

Here is the nucleus of your year's Science program. The group, given free rein and permission to stay after school, will bring honor and glory to its teacher at the next county Science Fair.

The younger teachers may worry about their meager scientific background, feeling insecure. "What if they ask ME?" is a common, fear-laden question.

The answer is obvious and it is best to put it across early in the year. When a child asks you the difference between alternating and direct current, you place a fatherly (or motherly) hand on his shoulder and make the following spiel. "Nick," you say, "I could explain their concepts to you in a few minutes. But honestly would this help you to learn?" You stop the beginning of an affirmative nod by hooking a finger under his chin, tilting his head back and looking him straight in the eye. "Of course not," you go on. "True learning must be the result of *your* labor. Nick, my boy, if you wish to know the difference between alternating and direct current you must [here you drop your voice and enunciate each word slowly and clearly] LOOK—IT—UP!"

This short speech repeated two or three times in September should keep you free of bothersome detail work throughout the year.

It should be pointed out that this group of Science's chosen people will inevitably develop a certain snobbishness and will club together to concoct solid rocket fuel and design elaborate oscilloscopes. To combat this the teacher must occasionally bring them down a peg. Listen carefully as they lecture the class. When they make a mistake in *grammar,* pounce like a tiger. That's what's the matter with scientists today. They talk lousy.

A Pip of a Pendulum

"*P*ROGRESSIVE" has many commonly accepted meanings—unless you're talking about education. When a businessman or a company is described as progressive it is thought to be complimentary; it means modern, foresighted, advancing with the times. But when a parent stops me and says, "Do you believe in progressive education?" I must be cagey. A mistake here will trap me and probably be quoted in the local newspaper because what the parent is really asking is this: "Do you believe in letting the kids do just what they please?" That's the public's idea of progressive education. The public wants education to be modern, foresighted, and advancing with the times, but not progressive.

Before John Dewey, things were different. First of all you walked to school—barefoot—in the snow. My grandfather told me that and he wasn't a man to lie—not while my grandmother was listening—which she wasn't on that occasion. And when you got to school, you sat, feet flat on the floor, and you *learned*. Boy, did you learn! You learned what it was to get sliced behind the ear with the ferruled side of a ruler. You learned the most becoming angle for wearing a dunce cap. You learned to stand when answering a question and to speak only when spoken to. You also learned how to read and write a little.

67

After Dewey, the pendulum began to swing away from strict discipline and toward a greater freedom of action. This pendulum has swung and swung and swung. By the time it finished swinging toward freedom in the classroom, there were hardly any classrooms left. Teachers, too, became quite scarce.

Of course the children greatly benefited from this technique. They learned to smear paint and break windows and stuff toilets full of geography books. And, since they were able to choose their own curriculum, they naturally chose those things which would enable them to carry out their life's work—namely the destruction of society. But they weren't frustrated!

By this time the public began to cry for the return swing of the pendulum.

Some cried, "Return sanity to the classroom."

Some cried, "Give the police back their night sticks."

Some cried, "To hell with understanding. Let 'em learn the multiplication tables the way I hadda."

And one damn fool cried, "Remember the *Maine*."

The pendulum has swung back again but not all the way. And don't think for one moment that the pendulum has stopped swinging. There's a strong group agitating right now for replacement of first grade with a class in pottery making.

In addition to the big pendulum, there are many smaller pendulums whipping back and forth across the landscape. Each subject area has its little clique of pendulum pushers trying to move it one way or the other.

Just the other day I was at a meeting of Home Economics teachers who are requesting that the new electric stoves be junked and the old coal ranges restored. Miss Shirtwaist, the Chairman of the Committee for Putting the Fire Back in Cooking, had this to say: "The pendulum has started swinging back. We women no longer want to depend upon an erotic [she meant erratic, I believe] transformer on some distant pole. Give us a few sticks of wood and a scuttle of coal and we'll put the fire back in cooking from whence it should never have been removed."

Education is not the only area that has pendulum trouble. The

68

Firstnationalcitybank of Firstnationalcity, Utah, has abandoned consumer credit. "The pendulum of consumer credit is a two-edged sword upon which we will all hang if we don't reverse its flight," said Mr. Frank Tightbuck, former head of the bank's credit department, who is good with credit but lousy with metaphors.

Nevertheless, it is in the field of education that the oscillating device made famous by Edgar Allan Poe creates the most havoc. First let's look at a comparatively new but frighteningly expanding group, the educational specialist.

You might point out that we have specialists in medicine, engineering, and management, so what's wrong with having specialists in education? Of course there's nothing wrong with it and indeed we do have many. We have the psychologist, the speech therapist, the home-school social worker, the reading consultant, the science consultant, the music specialist (vocal), and the music specialist (instrumental). All are helpful, all are dedicated, all are necessary, and all add to the teacher's burden. Don't look so surprised. While the addition of a specialist to the staff seems wholly in line with modern scientific thinking, it has two failings which are not readily discernible when the specialist is first hired. In fact the hiring of a new consultant is usually greeted by murmurs of approval by many staff members. Closer examination will show that approval is voiced only by the new teachers; the old-timers seem a little disgusted by the idea. That's because they have seen all those forms before.

Immediately upon entering his new job each and every specialist starts the mimeograph turning. With it he (or she) produces a mass of material designed to help him do his job. Each paper is addressed to The Classroom Teacher and on it The Classroom Teacher is asked to list, diagnose, indicate, formulate, outline, and review all the problems which are presently bugging her in the field of specialization being considered. Upon completion of this "preliminary survey" subsequent and far more intricate forms request "more detailed" information on your "most pressing problems."

For the psychologist we list nail biters and thumb suckers. We indicate IQ's, make anecdotal records, and observe social adjustments. For Music we list the tone deaf, the monotones, and the musically gifted. This must be done in duplicate since we have two music specialists. The Science lad would like to know all about the "interest areas" of the class to help him set up his program. The speech therapist wants the problems catalogued as to baby talk, lateral lisp, nasal pronunciation, etc. Reading would like to know how many are "above grade level" and how many "below grade level" and "how far above and below are these children?"

The trickle of forms which you expect to drop off after the initial surge shows no sign of diminishing. Instead the trickle turns into a stream as "evaluation and re-evaluation" and "progress reports" multiply like rabbits. June finds our stream a raging torrent as request after request pours in for information for promotion, retention, and summer schools.

September we're back in the same old rut. All the information given to the specialist last year is "obsolete in the light of recent findings." However "in order to facilitate the gathering of this needed information we have simplified the forms."

It's a good thing the forms are simpler. You'll need that extra time to fill out the forms sent round by the new Co-ordinator of Physical Education. Among other things he wants to know "the number of left-handed, left-eyed boys and girls listed according to their weight; the earned-run average of the three best pitchers in each grade, excluding kindergarten; and the number of teeth lost last year in girls' field hockey."

The pendulum has also swung in another area and up to the time of this writing shows no sign of reversing itself. I mean the Parent Teachers Association. In Grandfather's day parents and teachers got together only when the child entered school and when he graduated or was expelled, whichever came first. Between times all communication was via the report card. Today we have PTA meetings which are designed to bring parent and teacher together ostensibly for exchange of information concerning the child, but actually for mutual inspection.

Until this first meeting each has had a mental picture of the other transmitted by that most unreliable of all communicators—the child.

The child goes home and states flatly with no warning, "Miss Jones says I look like a slob and why don't you get me a clean dress."

What Miss Jones really said was, "Oh, Janet, you've gotten finger paint all over your nice dress. You'll have to get your mother to wash it right away." But mother's mental picture of Miss Jones has already begun to form.

Four days later Janet has another announcement. "Miss Jones," she says, "is sick of buying me ice cream every day. She says I should bring my own money."

Translation: "I'm sorry, sweetheart, I can't buy you ice cream. I'm sure your mother wouldn't want you to have two desserts."

A few weeks go by and Janet's mother is just beginning to feel that Miss Jones probably isn't *too* bad when the crowning blow falls. Janet, clothes muddy and disheveled, bursts through the door, dropping torrents of tears from red and swollen eyes. Her mother, a cold lump of fear rising in her breast, swoops the child into her arms and after fifteen minutes of soft murmurs and gentle kisses finally gets the story. "Miss Jones," Janet quavers, "hit me and knocked me down and I-I-I- didn't do nnnnothing." That does it! This is the end! Hit my child, will she! Well, I'm going to tell that old bat off at the PTA meeting tonight. If necessary I'll go to the Board of Education!

After dinner, as Janet's mother is dressing for the meeting, she rehearses her tirade against the sadist who has chosen to "pick on" her daughter. Her protagonist is clearly delineated in her mind. Miss Jones is an old maid in her early forties. Her style of dress is quite severe, almost mannish. She wears her hair pulled back displaying somewhat outsized ears and has steel-rimmed glasses which seem to emphasize her cold blue eyes. Her hands are like talons obviously made for mistreating little first-graders. Worst of all, she never smiles.

But communication is a two-way street and Janet in her role of cementer of home-school relationship has been helping Miss Jones

71

form her mental picture of Mrs. Thomas. For "Show and Tell" Janet brings in a shot glass and explains to Miss Jones and the class that "Mother drinks all her drinks out of this little glass."

She is equally eager to explain that her mother sleeps till " 'leven o'clock every day and I have to make my own lunch." That both the above stories were based on Mrs. Thomas' battle with a heavy cold Janet either didn't know or forgot to mention.

To reinforce the picture Janet casually in her conversation with the teacher is apt to quote her parents out of context. So Miss Jones is likely to hear such phrases as: "Tired of living in this filthy house" (said every Sunday when Mr. Thomas spreads the New York *Times* around the living room), or "I'll get a divorce" (a family joke—Mrs. Thomas murmurs it lovingly every time Mr. Thomas kisses her before shaving).

Now first-grade teachers are well aware of a child's wish to phantasize and Miss Jones leans over backward to believe only the best about the Thomas family. Nevertheless Miss Jones's picture of Mrs. Thomas is somewhat along these lines: A brassy blonde with a penchant for low-cut dresses. Her make-up is a little overdone and she smells faintly of whisky.

Mrs. Thomas, anxious to have it out with her child's teacher, arrives early. She glances into the classroom but sees only a young girl about eighteen, becomingly dressed and quite pretty, wandering among the desks. Probably waiting to talk about her little brother, who no doubt is also having trouble with this old shrew, she thinks. Mrs. Thomas waits outside the door tapping her foot impatiently. The young girl steps to the door and smiles—quite a nice smile Mrs. Thomas notices. "Good evening," she says. "I'm Miss Jones."

In an effort to cover shocked surprise Mrs. Thomas begins murmuring inane little nothings. Finally when she has adjusted her mental portrait she remembers why she came. Miss Jones is young and pretty but that doesn't disguise the fact that she is an inhuman monster who strikes little children. "Miss Jones," she begins quite severely, "I'm Mrs. Thomas. Janet came home today terribly upset."

"Oh yes," interrupts Miss Jones. "I do hope she wasn't injured."

"Well, no, not really, but I do think . . ."

"You see she started to dart out right in front of the bus and I just knocked her sprawling. I do believe I cried almost as hard as Janet did. I was so upset I didn't think to call. I do hope Janet explained it all to you."

A long pause as Mrs. Thomas shifts gears. "Why yes, yes, yes she did. She told me the whole story. That's why I was so anxious to see you, to thank you for what you did."

With understanding based somewhat tenaciously on the words of children, perhaps the PTA pendulum better remain where it is.

Nostalgia overwhelms me when I think about the great changes which have occurred in a field closely allied with education; although perhaps "allied with" might better be changed to "antagonistic toward" in many instances.

When I was in elementary school we had one or two men, usually with graying hair and pin-striped white overalls, who cleaned the classrooms, swept the halls, shoveled snow, put out countless barrels of ashes, cut grass, and still found time to catch the eighth-grade boys smoking in the toilets. These men were called janitors.

The qualifications for the job were few. They had to be able to identify a broom on sight. They had to have a strong antipathy toward children, and an ill-concealed dislike for all members of the teaching profession. It was considered an asset if their visages were completely devoid of any indication of a smile. Another thing which many seemed to possess was an ability termed by some "using *sotto voce* expletives" and by others "cursing under his breath." This skill was usually brought into play when the janitor was called upon to clean up a mess which teachers euphemistically call an "accident." It was obvious from the janitor's attitude and the barely discernible words that this occurrence was indeed not an "accident" but a deliberate attempt to interrupt his day's work. I knew that whenever I was sent posthaste to "get the janitor" he was to be found propped in a well-wired captain's chair raptly watching the rise and fall of the furnace flames. In my innocence I felt this to be the most important of all his duties and trembled for

73

fear of a boiler explosion whenever I was forced to take him from his post. It wasn't until eighth grade that I realized his post was the same even when the furnace was shut down. By that time my traumatic fear of asking a janitor to do anything was deeply engrained—and even today, as a teacher, I find it difficult to ask a janitor for anything. I usually send a child.

But styles in janitors, like other things in the field of education, have changed. He is not called a "janitor" now but instead is a "custodian." If there be more than one they are lumped together and called a "custodial force." The pin-striped overalls too have disappeared. (I wonder if they even make them any more.) Today's custodian is smartly dressed in gray or tan chino shirt and trousers and black tie. In some school districts this tie may be a snap-on bow. (In an attempt to maintain a high cultural atmosphere the more exclusive districts have banned the snap-on. Each member of the "force" must wear *hand-tied* bows. I say more power to them in their fight against mechanization.)

The word "force" in custodial force should not be taken lightly. It is difficult to measure accurately the power of an experienced custodian, but let me tell you, it is considerable.

A new teacher must show great respect for the principal, addressing him as Mr. —— and being careful to ask advice often and obey it faithfully. This is only common sense! Yet this same wise student of human relations will bustle into school on his second day of teaching and toss the custodian his car keys with these words, "Hey, I have two boxes of books in my car. Would you have them in my classroom by nine o'clock?" This kid will not last!

To treat a principal with respect is natural. But respectful treatment of the custodian in many cases must be learned. The relative value of these two most impotant people is worth investigating. It cannot be denied that the friendship of your principal is valuable when rehiring time rolls around. For helpful hints in classroom management or teaching techniques a principal is handy, but, ask yourself these questions: Will the principal hang a map for you? Will the principal carry a projector up from the basement? Will the principal repair your stapler? Will the principal help you change a tire?

These questions are purely rhetorical for it is perfectly evident that the friendship of a custodian is something to be cultivated. I would be the first to deny that a custodian is more important than the principal. Equal in importance, perhaps, but not more important.

One other area in which the custodian can be helpful is the matter of supplies. Both the principal and custodian have the same set of keys; therefore, it would be silly to bother a busy administrator with requisition slips and all the other red tape necessary to obtain supplies. It is much simpler to go directly to the source and have Sam drop off a gallon of green paint or a ream of drawing paper. Needless to say, in order to have this supply line operate smoothly a friendly relationship must be maintained. Speak humbly and carry a few cigars.

One very touchy point which should be thrashed out early in the teacher-custodian relationship is the matter of the actual teaching in the classrooms. A friendly constructive criticism is always welcome but Sam should be discouraged from the following:

1. He should never erase a word from the board which you have misspelled even if he does write it correctly.

2. He should *not* be allowed to comment on the accuracy of your Science lessons even if this comment consists only of a headshake and a low, "Tch! Tch! Tch."

3. He should refrain from showing the children the division method *he* learned in school. After all he only came to fill the soap container.

Such actions and comments by a custodian are quite apt to undermine completely the children's faith in their teacher, which is shaky at best.

The custodian of today seems to have a much nicer attitude toward children. He smiles often, snarls seldom, and seems well acquainted with modern psychology. This being the case, we teachers tend to look to him for help with our difficult problems.

If he comes along and finds you have parked Ted in the hall, no longer able to stand his making faces at you, Sam might well call you to the door and say, "If it's all right with you I'll take Ted downstairs. Maybe he can work off some of his aggressive attitudes by helping me burn papers."

Or again he may find you struggling with a group of poor readers. "Mr. Hannan," he'll say, "have you seen that new Reading series?"

"No," you answer.

"Well," says Sam. "It has an extremely high interest level and a low vocabulary. I think you'll find it ideal for that group of under-achievers."

"Gee, sounds great, Sam. I'll ask the principal about it tomorrow."

"Don't bother," says Sam. "I've got it right here in the hall. Let me explain this totally new concept for you."

Last week I visited my old school and there, still pushing a broom down the hall, was Mr. Haplan looking just as sour as if I had left only yesterday. I went to him hand extended, overflowing with nostalgia. "Gee, Mr. Haplan," I said, "you don't look a day older. Still school custodian, I see."

Mr. Haplan stopped sweeping but ignored the hand. "Who are you?" he snarled.

"You remember me, Joe Hannan. I spent eight years in this school."

"Then you ought to know I'm the janitor and not the other cussed thing you mentioned. And you ought to know better than to stop me when I'm sweepin' the hall!"

"Just wanted to say hello, Mr. Haplan." Now came the brag. "I'm a teacher now, you know."

Mr. Haplan squinted suspiciously at me. "You always did have them shifty eyes," he said as he pushed off down the hall.

You know he was wearing pin-striped blue and white overalls. They looked new. Maybe they do still make them.

The most far-reaching changes in education today are those having to do with electronic gadgets designed to make learning more pleasant and longer lasting. In the pedagogical double talk so loved by schools of education, these devices are familiarly termed AV. AV stands for audio-visual, the words being self-explanatory. To hear the modern teacher describe AV aids, one would think that the teachers of yesteryear had no such methods. But they did. They spoke, pointed to maps on the blackboard, and, in fact, were as audio-visual as the times permitted. But gradually, as the usefulness of electricity became more and more apparent even to college presidents, a whole new field of educational endeavor opened up. In this day of space flight and roll-on deodorants, the educators of America are not being left behind. There isn't a school of education in the land that would be caught without a sixteen-week course in Audio-Visual Aids. (I honestly feel that six weeks is plenty. In six weeks either you've mastered the machines or they've mastered you.)

I had never experienced the joy and reward of playing records on my own machine or of seeing those unforgettable scenes which I had captured in 16mm. full color flash across the screen. I had watched with envy the effortless, smooth manner with which my uncle handled his stereophonic hi-fi tape recorder. Breathlessly I saw him snap the reel into place, twirl a dial, flip a switch, and in less time than it takes to say Lee DeForest, have every beam in the house vibrating. I strained to hear his explanation of woofer, tweeter, and decibels and had left deafened but entranced by the wonderful world of electronics. And I had been entertained by friends with home movies, had watched them thread the machine, adjust the volume, and settle back to narrate the circumstances under which each scene was taken. Sure I had seen the show before, but what a pleasure it was to sit at the feet of a master and watch him handle the intricacies of the motion-picture projector.

So it was with the breathless air of a pilgrim approaching a sacred shrine that I found myself entering my first class in Audio-Visual Aids and there, lined up, glaring superciliously I felt, were the machines I hoped to command.

The motion-picture projector (4 models).

The tape recorder (6 models).

The slide projector.

The magic lantern.

The opaque projector.

So begins the struggle, man against machine with the instructor always in the background, hovering protectively, helpfully, alert for the sound of clashing gears or the smell of burning film. Before many sessions passed I found that this parental concern centers upon the machines. After all, he reasons, we have lots of teachers, but only four projectors.

At first it seemed a little complicated but all around me I saw people gaining skill and confidence. Look at that little old lady who is taking the course for renewal of a teaching certificate that expired in '08. Watch her tap the mike and murmur professionally, "Testing one-two-three. A-B-C." Watch that little freshman make a sprocket adjustment with a bent bobby pin. Obviously if these unmechanical types can master this business, I with my long years of experience changing tires in the gas station will have no trouble.

And so fear of failure which haunted me early in the semester was soon stilled as the instructor, in a confidential whisper with one arm draped protectively across a nearby Bell and Howell, told me that I was sure to get at least a "B" and to forget all that defeatist talk about taking the course again in the fall.

In September I came forth armed with knowledge, prepared for the modern era in education. Somehow, though, I had missed something. Somehow, despite the course, I had failed to acquire self-confidence—and the machines knew it. They sensed my basic inadequacy, the psychological deficiency which makes dealing with wired machines difficult—not impossible, just difficult.

My beginning ineptitude I passed off as arising from lack of practice. "Theory is all right," I told myself confidently, "but field experience is much more important." A few things went wrong but nothing of great note. Anyone could make a mistake threading a film strip projector. And the fact that I had gotten it wrong on ten consecutive tries was more a condemnation of the machine which was obviously obsolete, than of the operator who merely panicked.

The incident with the opaque projector was a little out of the ordinary but it seemed natural enough at the time to cool the machine with water when it appeared to be overheating.

My day of vindication finally came when the principal asked me to run a film program for the whole school. Knowing full well that the secret of success in a program such as this is preparation, I gave up my entire lunch period to prepare the equipment. It is well I did because it took me almost an hour just to open the screen. As a matter of fact I was just about to give up when a little girl from the third grade happened into the auditorium looking for her sneakers. Darn kid seemed to know quite a lot about movie screens.

Rushed a little now, with the time for the assembly fast approaching, I began to thread the projector. People began to file in just as I made the final loop on the pick-up reel. My own class looked at me quite proudly as I nonchalantly slammed all the little doors and stood relaxed, waiting for everyone to be seated.

The principal said a few words about the film, then nodded for me to begin. I opened the little doors, flicked on the switches, closed the doors, and sat down to enjoy the film. At this point the screen went blank along with my mind. I wrenched open the little doors just in time to see the film complete its trip backward onto the front reel. At this point something the AV instructor said came clearly to mind. "Always be careful to check your reversal switch."

I checked it now and by golly he was right. It was on reverse.

Trying to avoid the principal's eye I apologized for "operating difficulties" and commenced to rethread. It took quite a bit longer this time, probably because my fingers had grown fatter and sweat blinded me slightly. The audience seemed restless and began to whisper, then talk and finally to shout. But at last the job was done, I nodded to the light-switch tender, and the show began. I sat entranced with my own success until distracted by the principal, seated near the front, who seemed to be trying to attract my attention.

"Mr. Hannan," he whispered loudly.

"Yes?"

"The sound, please."

"What's that?"

"The sound, please turn up the sound." Even in the semi-gloom he saw my face redden. "This is a sound picture, isn't it, Mr. Hannan?"

"Yes, sir."

"Well?"

"I guess I forgot it. I'll take care of it right away." Then ensued another ten-minute wait till I found the sound equipment and hooked it up. At the end of the movie, as the children were filing out the principal again stopped. "Please don't forget to rewind that film. It has to go back in the morning."

"Rewind?" I croaked.

He was now beginning to lose some of the trust he had once placed in me.

"You did take a course in Audio-Visual Aids this past summer, didn't you?"

"Yes, but I must have been absent the day they talked about rewinding." At this point the little girl from the third grade stepped up on a chair and began to reverse the reels preparatory to rewinding.

"You two go ahead upstairs," she said. "I'll take care of this."

Of course this is behind me now. Then I was just a beginner, inexperienced, insecure. Now, I'm the AV co-ordinator of our entire school. I have a helper, a cute little fourth-grader with pigtails, named Trudie. I take care of all the major details, such as lugging the machines up to the second floor. After that I allow Trudie to take over the minor things such as adjusting the sound and threading the machines. Darn good little helper, too.

The Electronic Age is tough on teachers in yet another way. You hear a lot about teaching by television and its ever growing place in American education. In fact the talk is becoming so widespread it's beginning to make the teacher feel quite insecure. The "Why bother about hiring new teachers when you can have one TV educator take care of the whole school," attitude seems to be increasing in our country. Nevertheless, teaching by TV is still a very small part of the American educational scene. The thing that

80

worries me is commercial television and its effects upon teaching. You'll notice I said teaching, not learning. The burden that television places on the teacher must be sought in the areas of dramatics and history.

Let's take dramatics.

The true mark of a fine teacher is his ability to make his subject come alive, to create interest and a desire for knowledge. In this sense then, the teacher is an actor. He uses his voice, his movements, his expressions to hold attention and get his points across. In the dear dead days of yesteryear, this was a comparatively easy assignment. The unsophisticated elementary school child was well satisfied with a soupçon of drama. Any teacher who tended to "overact" either in manner or dress was termed a "screwball" and was treated as an imbecile child. Television has changed all that.

Today the average American child is a connoisseur of the dramatic art. Long hours of exposure to acting both good and bad have made him quite blasé. The day when you pointed out the difficult middle "a" in spelling "separate" by underlining is gone. To children, used to "getting the message" by a zooming close-up of the actor's expression, such mundane crutches as underlining have little or no significance.

As a result, teaching today has entered an entirely new phase. Dramatic presentation and eye-catching visual aids strive to gain the sated attention of the child. We work with multicolored pie sections to teach fractions and luminous maps to teach geography. The teachers themselves have taken to dressing for this purpose. A man will wear a bright Tartan tie in the hopes that such a conversation piece will lead to a more attentive study of the Stuart family's place in English history. Lady teachers appear wearing attractive print frocks, the print being the states of the Union, their capitals and chief cities. In the more progressive school systems, the female may sport blouses emblazoned with French or Spanish phrases—for the elementary school Foreign Language programs.

The act of teaching itself has become more and more dramatic. Each sentence and gesture is calculated to add to the over-all impact of the curriculum. In the day's plans you are apt to find little notes such as: "Walk slowly right to left carrying model of *Pinta,*" or "Mounting to desktop, shade eyes and peer while saying, 'I shall call the water Pacific because it is calm.'"

As the children become more and more inured to this type of teaching, the dramatic impact must become greater and greater. Soon we find a teacher flinging open the window and stating in loud, clear tones, "If everyone doesn't get one hundred per cent on this Arithmetic test I shall fling myself out."

This I feel is overacting but such steps are necessary in order to counter the dramatic methods used to educate by TV. Before you attempt to teach a Science lesson on the birth of a hurricane you must remember that you're in competition with Dr. Frank Baxter and Richard Carlson reinforced by a whole platoon of cartoon characters. The classroom teacher must suffer by comparison to such a cast.

But the problem of dramatics or the lack of them is secondary to the problems confronting History teachers. History is by definition a systematic record of past events. History, in so far as we can judge, is based on truth as recorded through the ages. Television History is another matter.

In the interest of selling more cigarettes or deodorant, the television writer resorts to the "based on" technique. As an example we'll take the undisputable fact of Paul Revere's ride. This historically valid seed must be expanded into a one-hour show. "The story as it stands wouldn't make a bad poem," mused the writers. "But we'll have to jazz it up a little if we want that spot on the 'Important Events in American History' program."

So they set out to make the story a little more "gutty," that is, they ring in sex. Ignoring Paul's marital status at the time of the ride, they give him a girl in Concord. Also this girl is being wooed by a captain in the British regulars. So Paul's ride, although ostensibly patriotic, is really done for much more basic reasons.

Paul comes in the back door of the girl's house as the redcoat captain enters the front. Then a scene ensues in which the dastardly acts of the dastardly British are pointed out. A fist fight follows. It would seem that swords would make a better scene but the writers' historical integrity is inviolate. Research has shown that Paul rode without sword and he won't be given one for the sake of drama. After a three-minute sequence in which every antique in the house is shattered, Paul lays the lobsterback low with a well-aimed pewter tankard. Then, amid a hail of bullets from arriving British infantry (the captain's amatory impatience causing him to lead his troops by a good few blocks), Paul and his girl, riding double on his wind-broken but gallant steed, make for Boston. They arrive just in time for the war bond kickoff banquet at the Old North Church which had been delayed because some prankster had hung every one of the Church's lanterns in the belfry. As the story ends Paul and his girl are being married in defiance of the British imposed three-day waiting period then mandatory in Massachusetts.

After that little story, the textbook version of Paul's ride seems drab even to the teacher, but in an attempt to rescue something, you question those who were lucky enough to see "Important Events in American History." "What did you think of Paul Revere?"

Everyone's eager to answer. "He was great. Did you see him bop that guy with the beer mug?"

"Yeah. And how about at Concord when he jumped off the barn that was on fire onto his horse! Wow!"

You try to steer things your way. "How about what happened at Lexington?" Blank stares till finally someone remembers.

"Oh yeah, that's where his horse lost the shoe and the blacksmith was a Story or Lory or something and Paul knocked him through the window onto the water wheel and down he went into the lake."

You nod. "Yes, that happened but how about the other thing at the bridge. You know when the farmers stood up to all those British soldiers. What did you think of those farmers?"

"They looked pretty corny to me, no uniforms or nothin'."

"Hey," chimed in another, "how about those British uniforms with the white strap. They were keen!"

"You shoulda seen it on my color set, red coats and all! Boy!!"

You see what we teachers are up against? Wagon trains which took two months to cross the Great Plains back in the 1800's now take thirty-two weeks with an occasional time out for a special feature. The Alamo rises and falls; Richard the Lion-Hearted shuttles back and forth between England and the Holy Land and every battle of the Civil War is reworked, its ending changed according to the birth state of the writer. So far television has confined itself to historical mutilation and has steered clear of other subjects. Still, if the shortage of material gets any more acute, the writers may feel a need to tamper with Math or Spelling.

"Let's throw a saddle on this and see how it rides. Everyone knows that two and two are four. But suppose—just suppose someone finds out that two and two are five. Get the significance here. Every calculation made by man since the beginning of time is off by one. See the picture? Now here's the . . ."

I've heard of an opening in a one-room school up near Hudson's Bay. It only pays eleven hundred skins a year (usually beaver) but I'm considering the idea.

The Annual Merry-go-round

P.S. 2
class 4-2

$\mathcal{T}$o EVERY teacher, male or female, the inexorable passage of time will bring a yearly crop of problems. Despite the famous unpredictability of children, a certain pattern of events will be followed. Some are imposed by tradition, some by the administration and some seem to be instinctive, imprinted upon the nervous system of generation after generation. All are inevitable.

They group themselves roughly into daily, monthly, and yearly happenings. A further breakdown will show them to be seasonal in nature, some adamantly so, while others seemingly occur accidentally. Spring, with its restless quickening of the blood, gives rise to the vast majority of these happenings. It is well that the teacher has had since September to prepare himself.

Daily

Through the years the daily routine of the schoolroom has been well established. After taking attendance you:

1. Read the Bible.
2. Say a prayer.
3. Salute the flag.

4. Sing a patriotic song.

You are given to understand that you then plunge headlong into Arithmetic while the children are rested and fresh.

NOT YET!

First you have lunch money to collect. This is really quite simple. A quarter from each child purchasing a hot lunch, slip it into an envelope and send it to the office. But wait a minute—Eddie has a five-dollar bill. Nothing to do but send him around to the other teachers looking for change.

As you begin to correct the Arithmetic homework, Eddie returns with his change. He had to go all the way down to the office and look, all they had were pennies. Eddie pays for his lunch and lurches lopsidedly away, pocket bulging. Don't for a moment assume you've heard the last of those pennies. Eddie keeps his handkerchief in the same pocket and his runny nose will insure that you'll hear from them again and again throughout the day.

Nine-thirty has come and gone and the Arithmetic homework still hasn't been corrected.

"Who," you begin, "has the answer for . . . ?"

But wait!

"Mr. Hannan," calls J. Peerpont Smith, "you forgot. Today is bank day."

And so it is.

Somehow, someone, sometime ago decided that the school was the place to teach thrift. (Might have something to do with the salary level of the teaching profession which would inspire thrift in anyone.) Cleanliness, good manners, and the value of money are virtues the home no longer seems responsible for. Instead the teachers make the pitch for Mr. Franklin's most quoted statement.

Even after all deposits are made, you're still not off the hook. Today is also the day you collect for the insurance and how about the money for the tee shirts that have "Mountain Side School" printed above the head of a snarling tiger? That has to be in by three o'clock.

This announcement results in a panic. Although you have faithfully carried out the dictates of the shirt company and have bellowed out prices and sizes twice a day since the first of the month, several of your charges seem not to have heard. Now, confronted with the specter of a chest unadorned by a snarling tiger, they clamor for the use of a phone. Mothers, it seems, will be interrupting the Reading period all morning. Let's hope they bring exact change.

Then, of course, there is the annual picture, taken either individually or in groups. Each child will be given a picture to bring home. If Dad decides it's a reasonable likeness, he will send in an appropriate amount.

We want [his note reads] only 2 of the wallet size, not six. The 5x8 is fine and could we please have an enlargement 15x24 for Grandma's birthday? Bill us accordingly.

Ten orders like that may well carry you entirely through Social Studies period.

Field trip money can be nerve-racking too. To get an over-all picture you find out the cost of a bus, divide it by the number in the class, and that's it, $1.75 apiece. Except that John and Frank don't want to go so that brings everyone up to $2.00—don't make that final. John and Frank will change their little minds six times between now and the big day. The wise teacher will prepare for such contingencies in advance. Fake the price a little. Charge a dime apiece over the expected cost. This will prevent you from being stuck and may result in some . . . Desk Money. This being the money left in the teacher's desk at the end of June. It accrues through miscalculation (see above), through unknown kids who came up to you on the playground, pressed $1.50 gratefully into your hand, and murmured, "I'll get it after the game. If I lose it my mother'll kill me" (presumably the latter has happened since the faces seen so fleetingly never appear to collect), and through honest children who give you all the money they find on the playground. The problem of what to do with this money is quite complex.

It certainly isn't the teacher's, no matter how you feel about possession and the law. You might buy a book for the school library or a film strip on the historical background of our monetary system. Better yet, let the staff pool its resources and buy a round of dry martinis. Imagine the expense if the schools had to hire a collection agency to handle its finances.

Another daily occurrence can best be shown by a short, stark drama.

Show and Tell

"Donna, darling," says Donna's mother, trying to remain calm as she peers into Donna's open lunch box, "Donna, dear, why do you have Daddy's toupee in your lunch box?"

"Oh, that's for 'Show and Tell,' Mother," says six-year-old Donna. "Don't worry it's his haircut one and he don't get his haircut till Saturday."

"Donna, you can't take Daddy's toupee to school."

"Why not?" asks Donna, her lip beginning to quiver a little.

"You just can't, that's all. Why don't you take that nice picture Grandma sent you from Niagara Falls?"

"Oh, sure, all the other kids bring in *their* swell things for 'Show and Tell' and I have to bring in a crummy picture of Niagara Falls. I want to take the toupee. I'll bet I'll be the only one to 'Show and Tell' a toupee this whole year."

"Once and for all you can't 'Show and Tell' Daddy's toupee. Now take the picture of Niagara Falls and be quiet."

The battle rages back and forth, neither female willing to give in till finally bus time forces Donna's surrender.

"All right," she cries as she boards the bus. "I'll 'Show and Tell' this crummy picture but I bet I get left back."

Mother wearily returns to the house, moves Daddy's cedar-lined Toupee Caddy to a higher shelf, takes two aspirin, and lies down with a cold towel over her eyes.

Back in the old days (a vague but useful measurement of time) a child was expected to come to school possessed of pencils, erasers, a ruler, paper, and his lunch. Anyone found to be carrying other implements, articles, or animals was deemed delinquent and sent to the principal for keel-hauling, banishment, or death by the guillotine, depending upon the number of past convictions.

In our modern educational methods, an attempt is made to connect the ofttimes dry content of learning with the interesting aspects of life which surround us.

One method of doing this is to encourage the children, especially in the lower grades, to bring in interesting objects, show them to the class and tell about them, hence the eternally coupled words, "Show and Tell."

"Show and Tell" has many results:

1. It motivates the children's learning, gains their interest, and can be expanded upon and used by an interested teacher.

2. It encourages children who are shy to take a more active part in classroom activities and gives them an opportunity to gain practical experience in speaking English.

Not all the results are salutary and it's necessary to point out that:

1. "Show and Tell" breeds a spirit of competition—not among the children as much as among the parents. It starts off innocently enough with an occasional sea shell or perhaps an oddly shaped whisky bottle. Eventually, though, someone in a moment of pride will press upon his or her child a treasured memento of some glamour and then we have the beginning of the race which eventually brings about scenes such as that with Donna and her mother. One father sends in a bat broken by Babe Ruth as he fouled out against Chicago in 1928. Another loving Dad, hearing of this and not to be outdone, sends in a football used in the Yale-Harvard game of 1933. The little girls, miffed at the attention these two objects got, go home and demand equally glamorous objects. Mothers begin to sharpen up their sights and soon we have a parade of objects that would do credit to a museum, ranging from a Paul Klee drawing to the original manuscript of *The Brothers Karamazov*.

This leads to a class war. The lower socio-economic group, being unable to compete at such a high intellectual level, turns to other more prosaic, but no less glamorous objects, such as four hub caps from a 1960 Dodge, or a sign which says, "Parking for Patients Only."

Finally though, the *pièce de resistance* arrives, carried in by two moving men hired for the job. It is a complete suit of armor which, due to some peculiarities of construction, is thought to have been used by Joan of Arc. This triumph stills the spirit of "Show and Tell" for the year but does not kill it entirely.

2. By its nature and purpose, "Show and Tell" is a lower-grade exercise. Kindergarten, first, and second grades are the natural realm of this device. I don't mean to imply that an upper-grade teacher does not welcome with joy an interesting object which brings home to the children the subject under discussion. But, unfortunately, the lower-grade teachers have done their job too well and a bad habit is hard to break. Long used to carting in a hodgepodge of items and being greeted by the teacher with thankful enthusiasm, they are quite nonplused when they reach fourth, fifth, and sixth grades and find those teachers less than gleeful at their proffered treasures.

"Well, here it is, Mr. Hannan," says Roger, dropping a ten-pound volume on your desk.

"What is it, Roger?" you ask.

"There it is, right on the cover."

"Chemical Engineering Catalog," you read, "published in 1928, huh, Roger."

"Yes, sir, ain't that great!"

"What are we going to do with it, Roger?"

"I don't know, Mr. Hannan, but you said yesterday that you love good books and that's a good book. It don't have one torn page."

"Fine, Roger," and resigning yourself to the inevitable, "show it to the class." This is typical of the unsolicited flow of litter that crosses a teacher's desk. They bring in their father's war medals ("He got this one for gettin' shot right in the heart.") or a discarded transmission from a Mack truck ("Can you imagine, they threw this on the junk heap. These things are worth a lot of MONEY."). This same group, which will team up to bring in the entire skeleton of a horse, will show up empty-handed when asked to bring in a picture from a magazine.

3. My third and last reason for being in opposition to "Show and Tell" in the upper grades is a penchant children have for animals as "Show and Tell" objects. This in itself is not bad but when they combine with a teacher who likes to put her "Show and Tell" show on the road, I begin to get annoyed.

It starts innocently enough. A child enters, carrying a small box and announces, "My teacher says I should show your class my rabbit." Rabbits are cute and you readily agree, thereby opening the floodgates of an unending stream of pets, most of which have one thing in common—lack of personality. When you've seen one rabbit you've seen them all, and that goes for frogs, turtles, and salamanders. Still, if you allow one child to show his turtle, how can you deny another child the same privilege? Once this craze for showing animals has begun the best thing to do is to relax until the storm passes—unless you're a positive thinker as I am. My little stratagem has completely freed my school from its annual influx of animals and is really simple to put into operation. You merely obtain a five-foot black snake, drape it around the neck of some lad who likes snakes, and send him around to the classrooms asking permission to show his pet. The repercussions from this incident will bring an immediate order from the office banning all live animal importation.

Of course you'll still have the sea shells, but no world is perfect.

One other thing will happen with great frequency in any elementary classroom. Perhaps it won't be a daily occurrence, but it certainly seems like it—at least till the teacher gains enough experience to handle the situation.

The announcement of the catastrophe usually occurs something like this. "Mr. Hannan!" The tearful scream reverberates throughout the building. "Mr. Hannan, somebody stole my father's pen. He'll KILL ME!!!"

You try to remain calm under such dire predictions. "Now, Joan, let's take it easy. It's probably in your desk somewhere."

"No, it ain't. I looked. It's gone I tell you and my father don't even know I took it. HE'LL KILL ME!!!" Her ending shriek reaches a note four octaves higher than the top note of an oboe.

"Now, now, calm down. How about your lunch box?"

"I looked."

"How about Lost and Found."

"Nope! Nobody turned it in. Some crook took it."

Now you start to worry. A couple of those older boys in the back do look a little shifty-eyed. What to do?

Well, there are many ways of dealing with this situation. We'll first look at the blindfold technique. You instruct the class carefully. "I'll stand in the hall holding the wastepaper basket behind me. You will come out one at a time, by rows, and if anyone has something that doesn't belong to him, he'll drop it in the basket. I won't know who it is and no questions will be asked."

So you stand, holding the basket till your arms ache and each child has made one trip (it is obvious from the giggles that Tammy, the class clown, has made at least three). You now have gathered a fine assortment of contraband including a cast-off peanut butter and jelly sandwich and that pair of sequin-decorated bricks that have been missing from your desk since Christmas. You have also gained the undying suspicion of the teacher across the hall into whose room you have been staring for the past fifteen minutes while your class passes behind you making disrespectful motions. What you don't have is Joan's pen.

Obviously this calls for action by the higher echelon. You dispatch Joan to the principal while keeping a wary eye on the rest of the class, hoping to catch one of them caching the pen away under his tongue. The principal arrives breathless and already well briefed by the tearful victim.

Now ensues a long lecture punctuated with many references to the Golden Rule to Good Citizenship, and to Playing the Game Right. A final offer is made. If the culprit will just admit his (or her) guilt no punishment will be forthcoming; if not, the whole class stays until the pen is found. At dismissal time no one has yet broken. More drastic action is called into play.

You can't search them bodily but you can have them clear out their desks and their pockets. This process takes about forty-five minutes. By then the secretary has notified you of six frantic phone calls from parents who've been waiting for their children. A small knot of angry mothers has begun to gather in the corridor outside the door of your room.

At 4:15 no progress toward a solution has been made but the principal is beginning to crack under the strain. He is just about to start his final plea when Joan's mother appears at the door. You hurry to explain the loss, telling her of your awareness of the gravity of the situation and its probable effect upon Joan's father. You begin to elaborate the scientific police methods used in the school when she interrupts.

"Oh, the pen. I *saw* her put it in her bag this morning and believe me I promptly took it out again. Why if she ever lost that pen HER FATHER WOULD KILL HER!"

You hurriedly dismiss the class and in turn are dismissed by both the principal *and* the superintendent of schools. A dive through an open window, a dash for the car, and you're away amid the smell of scorched tires before the mob can even decide whose pillow to use for feathers.

Every Thirty Days

Once each month we have report cards. Some more progressive schools have lengthened the reporting period to six weeks feeling that the effects of giving and receiving report cards are less traumatic if experienced at more widely spaced intervals. But every four weeks, six weeks, or eight weeks, everywhere in America, one of the following scenes takes place.

"Look, Ma," cries little Rodney Van Hepplewhite bursting through the front door of his home waving his report card. "Look, Ma, no *failures* this month!"

"Oh, darling! That's wonderful. Wait till we tell your father. I just can't believe it. No failures. Imagine that."

And that night when Mr. Van Hepplewhite comes home worn out from his stint at the colliery he finds his son's report card propped against his plate.

"Look, darling," says his wife pointing proudly. "Our son is a straight 'D' student at last."

"Yippee," cries Mr. Van Hepplewhite. "Ice cream and cake all around. We're all going to the drive-in as soon as I wash off the filth and grime of my stint at the colliery."

On the other side of town Jonathan Fitz Chippendale slinks dejectedly into the house through the rear window right into the arms of his father, a scrubbed-looking milkman who gets home early. "Well," says his father, "where is it?"

"Where is what?" asks Jonathan, pretending ignorance.

"You know what I mean. Today's the day report cards are sent home," says Mr. Fitz Chippendale, who always has these things figured. Jonathan shakes his report card down the leg of his pants and hands it to his father. "Just as I thought," cries the old man. "A 'B-plus' in English. Practically a failure."

"But, Pop, all my other marks are 'A's.' "

"What do you want, the *Croix de guerre?*" retorts the father, who is quite cosmopolitan.

"And I was out sick three weeks."

"No excuses, to bed without supper and no television for a month. I'll learn you."

"You mean you'll teach me."

"Huh?"

"I learn, you teach."

"You're practically a failure in English and you're going to tell me how to talk? Martha, bring the cat-o'-nine-tails."

"Now, Julius, it won't do no good beating the boy," says Mrs. Fitz Chippendale.

"It won't do *any* good, Mom," pipes Jonathan, who has a big mouth. " 'Won't do *no*' is a double negative."

"Hurry up with that cat-o'-nine-tails, Julius. I want my licks too," retorts Mrs. Fitz Chippendale in a kind voice.

96

What are report cards? Simply a method of showing the parent how well his son or daughter is accomplishing the work of the grade. It is a document of a private nature, meant only for the eyes of the immediate family. That's the theory. In reality, it's a club, the beating kind.

If your son comes home with all "A's," why keep it a secret? Blab a little. After all, look at his father. If the neighbor's son is a "C" student, that's all the more reason to spread the word. So you keep the card a few days, carry it in your lunch pail and show it around. Who worries about keeping it secret?

On the other hand if the following month sonny drops to "D—" the best thing to do is sign it and send it back. The less said the better. But the secret leaks and the neighbor, his silly smirk showing he already knows, asks you how your boy did this month. How did he find out? The kid talked.

It's part of their code to show each other their report cards and to speculate out loud just how badly they're going to "get it" when they get home. Even the kids who know quite well that their parents will be more than pleased pretend to worry.

The "D's" and below have certain uncomplimentary things to whisper about the teacher which they couple with terrible scowling glances. In vain you, as a teacher, point out that you had warned them. You mention that if only they'd done their homework and learned their division facts and paid attention in class this tragedy might never have happened. But their purpose remains adamant, you and you alone are responsible for their downfall. They go home and tell their parents that you "pick" on them.

What worries me is that sometimes the parents believe them without stopping to realize that teachers seem only to pick on the *poor* students. I have yet to hear an "A" student complain about being picked on, except by "F" students.

Modern report cards are different from those I remember. We got marks; 100 per cent was perfect and deviation from perfection was designated by lower numbers until you passed the point of no return, which was 70. Below that, oblivion. Your marks were arrived at by averaging all tests plus daily recitation, and you had no recourse when your average fell below the critical point. You also got marked for "Conduct" (sometimes called Deportment) and "Effort" (I wonder how they arrived at 68 in "Effort" without resort to telemetric devices?).

Today's streamlined report cards feature the alphabet, but parents keep asking, "But what is a 'C' in Numbers?"

Also the modern report card has a whole section devoted to the social graces. Such things as Co-operativeness, Leadership Ability, Followership Ability, and Aggressiveness (or Non-aggressiveness) are measured. This gives the parent whole new fields of worry which were never considered before. In order that the parents might give voice to their worries, the report cards have blank pages upon which a parent may pour out his hopes, his fears, and his ambitions for his offspring.

To the third-grade teacher:

Madam,
   Does this B in Spelling mean that Charlene won't make Bryn Mawr?

To the sixth-grade teacher:

Dear Sir:
   I wouldn't worry too much about Terrance and aggressiveness. He inherits it from his mother who has a terrible temper.

His Father

To a fourth-grade teacher:

Ma'm,
   If I had knowed you taut speling so lousy in this scool I woud have stood in east harbor which has darn good scools.

C. Taxpayer.

The latest innovation in reporting to parents has done away entirely with report cards. Instead the parent is invited to school to talk over the child's progress. By using this technique, the teacher can get a picture of the home situation and a parent can size up the teacher. It is safe to assume that a mother who starts the conference by asking, "What grade is Bobby in now?" won't be helping much with homework. By the same token the parent is bound to distrust a teacher who starts by saying, "I suppose you're here to discuss that rotten kid of yours."

Our methods of reporting and our report cards have changed through the years. One thing hasn't changed, though, and that's the treatment report cards get from the children.

You give out report cards at 2:57. At 3:02, Pierre is at your desk, face stricken with fear.

"Mr. Hannan."

"Yes, Pierre?"

"I lost my report card."

"You couldn't have lost your report card, you've only had it five minutes. How did it happen?"

"Well, I stopped at the boys' room on my way out and when I flushed . . ."

"All right, Pierre, I'll give you another one."

Then there's the problem of who signed the card. "Who signed your report card, Milton?"

"My mother."

"Oh? Well, this signature doesn't look anything like the one she signed last month."

"That's because of her arm."

"Her arm?"

"Yeah, she broke it and has to sign left-handed."

"Why didn't your father sign it?"

"He can't write."

"That's silly. He wrote me a note just last week."

"Oh yeah, he can write notes. It's just his name he can't write."

The methods used to get report cards in condition to return to the teacher have always intrigued me. First, they must be kicked all the way home. Second, they are always presented at the table during a meal, else why the butter stains? Third, they are held under hot water so the ink runs. Fourth, they are kicked all the way back to school. Report cards are terrible things. They create anger, sorrow, fear and pain—especially among teachers.

99

The Dog Who Comes to School

Dogs usually come to school in the fall. During the long summer days following his young master has become habitual. He sees no reason to change just because his master is wearing a tie, and his master sees no reason to chase him home. Why spoil a beautiful friendship?

You might assume from the above that it is always the same dog who comes to school. After five years of chasing dogs around inside school buildings, I can tell you it isn't the same dog—it just looks the same.

This dog is generally somewhat shaggy, hair long but not too long. It usually is multicolored with white patches prominently displayed. There is something about it that smacks of terrier and yet its ears are definitely hound. On the other hand, its front legs have a distinct resemblance to the improbable appendages of the Basset. Its tail is long and, in contrast to its body, is smooth-haired.

Perhaps I am being needlessly explicit if I point out that this animal's blood lines are mixed, if not to say snarled. This fact brings up an interesting point. I have noticed that a dog which follows a child to school is never a pure breed. Why? Could it be that pure breds are snobs and feel superior to the public school, condescending to follow a child only if the child attends a private school? Or perhaps well-bred dogs are confined more to the house and find no opportunity to attend school other than obedience training school? Or it may be in the breeding itself, the mongrel being of mixed parentage feels drawn to democratic camaraderie of the school grounds where he will be made to feel welcome no matter how muddy he might be.

And that brings up another intriguing aspect of this whole problem. Dogs who come to school are always muddy—even when it's not raining. A mud-covered dog can make quite an impression at school to say nothing of the impression he makes on the teacher's dress, the principal's trousers, and the custodian who has to run and clean up all those muddy impressions.

The issue that remains completely shrouded in mystery is how the dog enters the school. According to the accounts of the children, this happy-looking half-breed possesses all the wiles of a Jimmy Valentine and the animal cunning of Old Reynard. He evades their frantic efforts to corner him and somehow manages to pry open the heavy outer doors and enter the sacred precepts of the temple of learning. His progress through these hallowed halls is easy to follow—just listen for the delighted screams of the children as they joyfully chorus, "Oh boy, there's a dog in school!"

Their happy effusiveness is not shared by the teachers who, naturally suspicious, are further estranged by the disreputable appearance of the genial visitor. Then, too, it's always well to keep a desk between a set of muddy paws and a newly pressed suit or a pair of nylons.

No matter how the animal enters, the problem is to remove him from the premises as speedily as possible. The usual ineffective noises such as "Shoo" and "Go home," accompanied by the nervous brandishing of rolled-up newspapers and genuine cowhide brief cases, are useless. The teacher feels this is an administrative emergency and makes no concentrated effort to oust his new associate.

Instead a terse note is sent to the office.

There's a dog in school.

Signed,
Nervous

The administrator, ever alert, makes a typical administrative move and rings for the custodian, the reasoning here being that since his floors are being marred by muddy pawprints he has the most to gain by tossing the culprit out.

The custodian, however, although possessing a strong aversion to polishing floors, has an even deeper aversion to acting as bouncer for stray dogs and so states.

In the meantime, the dog, taking advantage of the impasse, has been wandering around, greeting old friends, visiting classrooms, lifting his leg against the teachers' desks, and otherwise behaving as would any other red-blooded American canine in similar circumstances.

It is at this juncture that the situation begins to clear up and in clearing up begins to involve me directly. For the past half hour or ever since the dog managed to break into the building, I had been hearing rumors to the effect that said dog belonged to Dexter Higgins, a boy in my class (for five years every dog which has visited the school has belonged to a boy in my class, except once when it belonged to a girl in my class). When finally the dog finds its way into my classroom, it yips loudly and bounds happily into Dexter's lap. My suspicions are confirmed.

"Dexter, is that your dog?"

"Yes, sir," states Dexter.

"That's fine. What's his name?"

"Lassie."

"Oh, it's a girl dog."

"No, sir, it's a boy dog."

"How did he get to school, Dex?"

"I guess he followed me, sir."

"You didn't encourage him, did you?"

"Yes, sir, I tried to encourage him, but he came anyhow." Ignoring the opportunity for fruitless discourse this exchange presented, I jump into the solution of the problem of the moment. "Look, Dex," I suggest, "why don't you just take Lassie down to the door and put him outside? He'll find his way home."

"Gee, Mr. Hannan, he'll get hit by a car!"

Now this dog is wily enough to survive on the busiest parkway on a Sunday afternoon in summer, but who can place a boy's dog in jeopardy?

"Well, what *can* we do with him, Dexter?"

Hopefully, "I could take him home."

"How long would that take you?"

"Oh, I guess I could get there and back in about two hours."

"Now, Dexter, you only live over there by the river."

"Yeah, well . . . I guess I could make it there and back in about an hour . . . if I hurry."

"O.K., Dexter, stop at the office and tell the principal you're going to take Lassie home, and, Dexter, please hurry."

102

"Yes, sir, I sure will."

"And listen, Dexter, stop at the boiler room and get a piece of rope so Lassie doesn't get away again."

"Oh, you don't have to worry about that, Mr. Hannan," says Dexter reaching into his pocket. "I've got his leash right here."

What kind of a day has it been? A day like any other day, full of those little unexpected happenings they never tell you about in teachers' college.

The Field Trip

One particularly horrible annual event, which all teachers experience, is the field trip.

In the years before I started teaching, when intimidated by the predictions of my friends, all of whom seemed well acquainted with "blackboard jungles," "switch-blade knives," and "irrational parents," I always had an answer. "Well," I used to state confidently, "if the going gets too rough and I need a day off I can always arrange a field trip."

This flight into naïveté was successful for six months—or until I took my first field trip. Dealing with thirty lively sixth-graders within the confines of a well-designed classroom can be nerve-racking; still the walls lend a certain structure to the situation which is comforting. Spread these same thirty over four floors of the Museum of Natural History and a difference will be immediately apparent.

ARRANGING FOR TRANSPORTATION

This is usually taken care of by the office. A date is set, the principal calls the bus company, and you forget the whole matter—until the big day.

Thirty eager, expectant children are seated, clutching lunch boxes and comic books (never mind about the eyestrain, it helps keep them quiet). At five minutes to nine you begin pacing back and forth in the hall, glancing out the window once every eight seconds. Nine-o-five and it suddenly occurs to you that you never verified the bus. You appoint a monitor, being careful to keep panic out of your voice, and dash for the principal's office.

"The bus? Oh, yes," he says. "Nine-thirty Mr. Jones said."

"Mr. Jones? Who is . . . ?" Of course, Mr. Jones, the other sixth-grade teacher whose class is also going on the trip. You trudge back to your class, shaken but relieved and still, gnawing at the back of your mind, is the doubt. Maybe the bus won't come.

At 9:20 the bus pulls into the yard. Fortunately you are standing in the doorway of the classroom and are able to beat back the mad rush with only minor casualities. "All right, now, everyone sit back down!" Reluctantly they comply with your request.

"Now," you begin, "how about those rules we outlined for ourselves. Remember the one about staying in line, and the one about not running, and the one about being polite and not pushing and the one . . ."

"Hey, Mac." It's the bus driver leaning in the window. "Whatcha say, huh, I gotta schedule to keep, ya know."

You lead the mad dash for the bus being sure to call out in a loud clear voice, "I get a seat by the window."

ON THE BUS, GOING

The American people have come to expect a certain amount of surliness from their taxi drivers, train conductors, and bus drivers. In the case of a bus driver who takes a group of sixty children and two confused adults into the big city, such surliness can be justified. Therefore, it is well to speak politely, to ask if there is anything this particular driver doesn't like, and to mention in passing that: "I drove a school bus when I was in college." This last is, of course, a blatant lie but it does help to establish the feeling that you're regular and before you went into teaching *did work* for a living.

104

The driver may make a few simple requests:

1. "Don't open the windows!" (It's too late since every window in the bus already has been opened despite the thirty-seven-degree temperature. Your best bet is to promise they will be closed immediately.)

2. "Don't sing."

3. "Keep 'em quiet." This is impossible, but agree anyway. (My last driver was quite unique: "I don't give a damn what they do as long as they don't sing, 'I've Been Working on the Railroad.'" I liked that man.)

The bus will pull out amid children's jeers and catcalls directed toward their less fortunate classmates who have to spend the day in school. You, too, are aware of a few jeers and catcalls directed at you by the teachers who don't have to go on a field trip.

You settle down for the ride into the city. If each child brings one comic book and then swaps for others, this portion of the trip can be quite serene. For those who become ill from reading on a moving vehicle, it is well to provide cardboard boxes. For those who are bored by comic books or who are reading below grade level, other diversions are present such as:

1. Eating lunch (saves carrying it later).

2. Eating candy (watch that one, he'll turn green about 11:02).

3. Chewing gum ("Look, Mr. Hannan, I've got three whole packs in my mouth at once!").

And so the city.

AT THE MUSEUM

You must always carefully plan a trip to a big museum. Get a floor diagram, explain it to the children, point out the things they are going to see so that they will recognize them when the time comes, and above all, schedule carefully. The following will show you what I mean.

9:30—Arrive Museum (you'll have to change this because the bus was later than you figured).

105

9:30–10:00—Hall of Mammals (you'll have to move the time up a little since it takes to 10:32 to locate the Hall of Mammals).

10:00–10:30—The Hall of Ocean Life (better rush them through this; the Planetarium show starts at 11:30 and it is now 11:09).

10:30–11:00—Birds of the World (skip this, still haven't found the damn Planetarium and the show starts in six minutes).

11:00–11:30—Gems of the World (can't make it).

11:30–12:30—The Planetarium.

On a school day every large museum seems to be visited by thousands of children. Each group moves about independently and there is little evidence of strain—until they reach the Planetarium. Here myriad groups converge and here the teacher's nerves are stretched to the breaking point. The lights dim, a well-modulated voice begins the lecture and is soon drowned out by the rustle of paper bags, the crunch of popcorn, and the plaintive wails of the famished, "When do we eat?"

Even the novelty of learning that on the moon they would weigh only eight pounds, nine ounces, can't divert them for long. "If I don't eat soon," states one little boy, "I ain't gonna weigh eight pounds, nine ounces on eart."

12:30–1:00—Lunch. The lunchroom is another point of convergence. Even the most efficiently run cafeteria will occasionally run into a bottleneck. When this bottleneck consists of five-hundred hungry children in assorted sizes, the problem becomes catastrophic. Glares from the guards will not keep them quiet while waiting in line, and even the best-run museum will occasionally find the remnants of a surreptitiously eaten sandwich among the shrunken heads.

As you file toward the lunchroom you'll pass doors marked BOYS and GIRLS and it may occur to you that no one has "been" since before class this morning. "Does anyone have to go to the bathroom?" you announce in a loud voice, and find yourself looking directly at the fierce female who's been trying to muscle her class past yours. Your blush doesn't deter your class; they all have to "go."

106

1:00–1:30—The American Indian Room. (Forget it. It's 2:00 o'clock now and the bus driver has given strict instructions: "I gotta leave here two-forty-five the latest." Better just head for the last place scheduled.)

2:00–2:30—Souvenirs. The souvenir counter is jammed and your group adds to the chaos. Your best bet is to stand back and let nature take its course. Remember, you can't be at peak efficiency every moment.

So far the day has gone along quite smoothly. No one has been lost for more than fifteen minutes, only two people were sick, and there was just one small fight instigated by that particularly nasty bunch from Spring Valley. The trip is drawing to a close and it is natural to let down a little. At this point you begin to make mistakes —really big mistakes—with consequences.

Mr. Jones, your fellow teacher, has a fine suggestion. "Why not have the bus come around and meet us here? That way we won't have to walk around the building." A good plan. He sets off through the building and you are left in charge of the sixty children.

At first it isn't too bad. Your group is lost among the milling throng, but gradually the mob begins to thin out. You approach the guard in a friendly fashion, trying to show you're sympathetic to the burdens of his job (and incidentially to try to divert his attention from your group, which seems particularly rowdy). "Pretty rough day for you fellows."

"You're damn right," he grunts, refusing to be diverted.

"I guess you don't have many days as crowded as this?" You're immediately sorry you asked.

"Every day is like this," he says, "but I'll tell you this. This is the noisest bunch this year." He seems to be glaring pointedly at your children. You look out, note that the bus isn't in sight, and decide to try one more gambit.

"You know, I worked as a part-time museum guard when I was in college." By his silent scorn you realize he has spotted this for just what it is, another blatant lie. "All right, people," you announce, "we'll wait for the bus outside."

Outside it has turned quite a bit colder, and since all coats were left on the bus, complaints are soon heard. You decide to walk around to meet the bus. Nothing to lose here, the driver has to come this way. But, you don't meet the bus. You walk around the building and into the parking space. The bus, the driver, and Mr. Jones have all disappeared. The feeling of being all alone is never so deadly as when you are stranded in the heart of a big city, on a late fall afternoon, with sixty children.

"Surely," you think, "Mr. Jones wouldn't go home without me. Unless of course he came back, found the bus gone and a scathing note of resignation from the driver. In that case, thinking of a subway trip with sixty coatless children, he might just be chicken enough to . . ."

It's best to shake such traitorous thoughts from your mind and concentrate on solving the immediate problem. You call the group together and speak right from the shoulder.

"Now, I know we're all cold and the bus seems to be missing. You're all grown-up children and I know I can count on you standing here quietly, in line, while I go look for Mr. Jones and the bus. Can I trust you?" Their fervent chorus in the affirmative gives you the courage to leave them and start back around the building.

As you look back from the corner they don't seem too bad. Except for the two boys breaking that branch off the tree and the three girls being chased by that muscular-looking lad from Mr. Jones's class, everything seems under control.

Your hurried dash back around the building is in vain. No bus, no driver, no Mr. Jones. The souvenir counter is deserted. Our guard, smiling now, states that he has seen neither a bus driver nor a harried-looking teacher. Back out the door and around the block the other way, ignoring your pounding heart and knotted stomach. WHERE COULD THEY BE? You round the corner into the parking lot. NOW THE CHILDREN ARE GONE!

You slump to the ground, a completely broken man.

At this point a strident horn begins to sound and sixty voices shrill your name. "MR. HANNAN! MR. HANNAN! HERE WE ARE! WE'RE HERE!" Mr. Jones is kind enough to assist you aboard the bus murmuring something about "One way street" and "We must have missed you." The driver, too, is murmuring something. "Stupid jerk! Who the hell's gonna explain *this* to my boss?" Relief flooding through you, you slump into a seat. Home, James!

ON THE BUS, COMING HOME

The comic books have all been read and now's the time for song. What songs? Any songs as long as they can be sung loudly and with constant repetition. A truly successful field trip song is one which can be started as the door of the bus closes for the return trip and finished when you pull up in front of the school. This can be varied by contests, boys against the girls, as to who can:

1. Sing louder.
2. Sing shriller.
3. Hold a note longer.
4. Whistle "The Marine Hymn" the worst.

The teacher may attempt to control the situation by patrolling the aisle, motioning for silence or at least moderation. You may also ignore the piteous moans of the driver, let the children have their head and hope you won't get the same driver next trip.

THE AFTERMATH

The last parent has pulled away, the bus has long since returned to the garage, its driver somewhat appeased by a $5.00 tip. You and Mr. Jones shake hands in silence and start for home. On the morrow, though, things will be different.

"How'd the trip go?" your fellow teachers ask. "Fine." (You're still blatantly lying.) "A little scheduling trouble but nothing to amount to anything." They nod knowingly. They, too, have taken field trips and they, too, realize that any attempt to discuss them frankly would lead to the abandonment of the whole business.

Back in the classroom the next day the children, those who have managed to attend, are quite vocal about the trip. Deciding this is a fine time for a language lesson, you pass out paper and on the board write the title of the composition: "My Impression of the Museum."

They all do a fine job. Twelve were amazed by the hot-air hand dryers in the rest rooms. Eight were flabbergasted by the fact that a stream of water from the drinking fountain near the Hall of Mammals could be made to reach the opposite wall. Six were fascinated by the Coke machine that made change. Three were irritated at a cafeteria that would dare charge ten cents for such a small amount of soda. One little boy thought the Planetarium was "pretty good." Unanimity reigned on only one question: "When are we going on our next field trip?"

The Christmas Play

Right smack in the middle of every winter comes Christmas. At best this time of year is extremely trying for teachers. Visions of sugarplums have considerably diminished the attention span of even the best students in the room. In addition to the usual run of hobby parties and Christmas decorations, at least one class will be putting on a Christmas play. And at least one teacher will be hypertensive. It's not as if he hadn't been warned.

Casually, in September, the principal mentions that "Mr. Hannan's sixth-grade class will give the Christmas Play this year." Your heart stops for a moment but complacency, engendered by the intervening months, soon takes over and your pulse returns to normal. Who can think of Christmas when they haven't played the World Series yet? October comes, and while watching Miss Creighton's first grade sail shakily over the raging Atlantic in search of a new route to India, you firmly resolve to pick a Christmas program tomorrow. Next Monday for sure.

Things being what they are, it isn't until the members of Mrs. Smith's fourth grade begin to step from a cardboard *Mayflower* to a papier-mâché Plymouth Rock that you begin to break out in a cold sweat. Jumping Reindeer! Christmas is only a month away!

Those Broadway producers are nothing! What do they know of

the true frustrations of the theater? What do they know of tempera-
mental leading ladies and sensitive leading men? How can they
speak of opening-night jitters, of last-minute cast replacements, of
frantic rewriting the day before the opening? I ask, above all, what
do they know of the critics? Have they ever played to a group of
their classmates?

Listen, Mr. Producer, and I'll tell you of the true test of love for
the theater. I'll speak of the crucible from which emerges some of
the outstanding theater lore of our times.

Listen, sir, and I'll tell you of the SCHOOL PLAY!

First the search for a vehicle worthy of the class's talents. Here's
an area in which the professional has a huge advantage compared
to the selector of a school play.

If Arthur Miller writes a play in which there are eight characters,
someone goes out and hires eight actors. If William Gibson writes
a play for two characters, someone goes out and hires two actors.
On the other hand, I must fit my play to the class. And I might here
note that a play written for nineteen girls and thirteen boys is not
common in the history of the Western theater.

So you begin. You ransack the magazines. This year's and last's
and back to the plays depicting the evils of drink (very popular in
the twenties). Those which are interesting have too few characters.
Those which contain the correct number of characters (give or take
a few) are too expensive to costume and, those which are easy to
cast and cheap to costume involve building a set whose central piece
is a half-size replica of the Colosseum.

About this time you fall into an ever yawning trap. Having
arrived at a point beyond which desperate measures are necessary,
you decide to let the children write their own play.

At first you let the whole class participate, the feeling being that
those who aren't able to write a coherent sentence will at least be
able to contribute a few ideas. Here a strange metamorphosis takes
place. Somehow the ideas of those who can write get mixed up with
the incoherencies of those who can't and the whole thing comes out
sounding like "The Blue Danube" played backward. Nevertheless
a little touch-up here and there, a bit of rewriting by the teacher, and

your democratically produced play is ready for the boards. One minor point. The money necessary to build the set and costume the characters in this play could keep three road companies of *My Fair Lady* going for six months. Don't throw it away. Maybe you can sell it to one of those teachers' magazines. I got $7.00 for the last one I put my name on.

With Christmas only three weeks away, you now must resort to further desperate measures, perhaps even chicanery or in extreme cases bribery. You must trap the music teacher into doing "your play." This isn't easy since up till now you've given her to understand that Music must stand second to the true purpose of public education which, of course, is Physical Education.

You can soothe your conscience by such rationalization as: "It's easy for her, she can work those extra kids into a great little chorus."

"After all, Miss Little, the true spirit of Christmas can only be caught by music." No need to resort to bribes however. To her eternal credit, Miss Little jumps at the chance to put on a Christmas program.

So, three weeks before the big day you begin rehearsals. All does not go well. First of all the children must learn the songs. This involves class drill, written assignments, notes to parents, threats of retention, or in really recalcitrant cases, even demotion. Eventually all but three learn all the words. These three have learned to fake lip movements which coincide quite well and are hard to detect.

Next comes the clinkers (a Latin term denoting children who are tone deaf). Giving our music teachers every credit, I must say that during the school year they work hard doing remedial music with these youngsters. But, with opening night less than three weeks away, we have no time for the niceties. We'll assign them more important parts like Curtain Puller or Audience Counter or Page Turner (for the latter, we try to obtain a tone-deaf child with some knowledge of music—not an easy combination).

Picking the clinkers out requires a keen ear, psychological insight, and rubber-soled shoes. You see, these children are in sixth grade. They've been through the mill. They've been Page Turners

112

and Curtain Pullers before and this time they're determined to sing, tune or no tune. You have to stalk them.

The usual procedure is for the music teacher to lead them in a rousing marchtime song hoping that their enthusiasm will give them away. As they sing the classroom teacher circulates nonchalantly among them smiling, seeming to join in the fun but really out to trap the unwary. Most are picked off quite soon, carried away by an exuberance unmatched by ability. A few, schooled in the ways of musical plays, watch you out of the corners of their eyes. As you approach the seat of discordance it suddenly ceases. You watch for unmoving lips but everyone is happily mouthing the words. You can't tell who isn't singing. Patience and weariness caused by over-long rehearsals will result in the eventual fall of all but one of the non-harmonious singers. This one will defy detection and will eventually be accepted with the hope that the loud pedal on the piano will cover up most of his *faux pas*. You might go through life never knowing who the culprit was but I doubt it. I'm sure the day after the play he'll come up and say, "You know, Mr. Hannan, that's the first time I've ever been allowed to sing on the stage." He's the one all right.

On one score we of the scholastic theater do have an advantage over Broadway. The jobs of costume designer, wardrobe mistress, make-up artist, etc., are taken over by the ladies of the PTA. With no thought of recompense either monetary or honorary (except perhaps mention in the newspaper), these good people work from morn till night, cutting, fitting, basting, sewing, and striving to overcome by sheer dressmaking skill the problem of changing sixth-grade girls into angels and boys into shepherds and kings. The end effect is startling and brings tears to the eye of the teacher, who up till now has seen his charges only as a series of small boys and girls somewhat deficient in the knowledge of the finer things of life such as the 100 division facts.

The days fly by at a tremendous rate. At the start some attempt is made to complete the usual daily assignments, but toward the end pretense is flung aside and all concerned devote themselves full

113

time to setting up the stage, decorating the auditorium, preparing the programs, and, of course, rehearsing. Tempers, especially those of the adults, grow increasingly short and it is not unusual to find that on the morning of the dress rehearsal no one is speaking to anyone except in the line of duty.

DRESS REHEARSAL

Dress rehearsal is the first uninterrupted run-through of the show. The stage manager, in charge of getting the cast on and off, on cue, has been selected for his keen sense of the theater, his knowledge of music, and an equanimity which can only be described as hair-trigger. Also you're the only adult available.

All goes smoothly for the first half hour. People enter on cue, mouth their words with a minimum of giggles, and step on each other's trailing robes only occasionally. Even a last-minute insertion of a new soloist, completely unbeknownst to the stage manager, causes only momentary panic.

Still, as the show moves along he begins to notice a certain uneasiness, a glazing of the eyes of more than one of the large cast. Temperatures behind the footlights mount steadily and finally the inevitable happens. One of the topmost choristers, overcome by excitement, heat, and the lack of breakfast, passes out and hurtles to the floor, his fall luckily broken by intervening angels and shepherds. Noting the care and solicitude lavished on this poor unfortunate by the principal and the school nurse, who have dragged him into the wings, a hysterical reaction sets in and gaps begin to appear among the ranked angels and chorus at an alarming rate.

The music teacher, bravely ignoring the bodies strewn like autumn leaves about her feet, carries on. At this critical juncture the day is saved by a little first-grader who plaintively inquires in a loud voice heard throughout the auditorium, "Miss Jones, when they all fall off can we go?"

Oh, well, dress rehearsals aren't supposed to go smoothly anyhow. Ask any producer.

114

THE BIG NIGHT

The big night finally arrives. Some are eager, some frightened, some joyful, others sad (tomorrow they have to go back to Arithmetic); and one at least has the distressingly imminent signs that his annual attack of duodenal ulcers is about to commence. Still he manifests a cool exterior, managing to keep panic from his voice as he issues last-minute instructions as to behavior in the halls, level of voice that is expected of the group waiting to go on (absolute silence), and reminding that angel not to scratch herself on stage —which she does anyway. He attempts to speak persuasively to the boys who resent the application of lipstick, pointing out that even Marshal Dillon must wear make-up while performing. Only once is he seen to lose control and well he might. One of the shepherds (a profession notorious for its practical jokes, as witness the experiences of "The Boy Who Cried Wolf") has locked three of the angels in the girls' lavatory. Our calm, cool, and collected stage manager is seen dashing wildly down the hall screaming for Mr. Lumster, the custodian. He returns ashen and breathless, dragging Mr. Lumster, who is even more breathless, since he is nearing his seventieth birthday. The problem has been resolved, however, by one of the imprisoned angels who forced the lock with the end of a wire coat hanger, which, by the way, was doubling as a halo.

The cue music is finally heard, and calmly with no sign of inner turmoil, the children file on stage. All are in place, their voices swelling the first song. Our stage manager, thinking to take a moment of needed relaxation, returns to the classroom. There the effects of the past week of strain begin to tell and he begins to hallucinate. He thinks he sees two of the three kings calmly playing checkers. Thinking to dispel the whole scene, he speaks.

"What," he asks, "are you two doing here?"

The startled look on their faces kills any hope that they are figments of a disordered mind.

"Oh!" asks one. "Did everybody go?"

115

A wild dash to the auditorium and two somewhat disheveled kings, turbans askew, take their places as their parents writhe in helpless embarrassment.

The final curtain falls and amid thunderous applause the cast takes its bows. Then comes a frantic scramble to the classrooms. Desperate scrubbings by the boys to remove all vestiges of femininity while the girls seize this opportunity to repaint lips, granted lipstick for this one night. Parents arrive, extend congratulations and finally drag reluctant offspring away.

Yes, Mr. Broadway Producer, we know the heartbreaks and rewards of the theater, don't we? We know the planning, the work that goes into producing a play. We know the agonized pacing, the frantic revisions that precede the final version. On one point, though, we differ. You might know failure. I have never had an unsuccessful production.

On the other hand, you probably have never had to teach the relationship between improper fractions and mixed numbers on the morning following opening night.

The Spring Musicale

While the Christmas Play was a rousing success, the Spring Musicale has an ingredient that makes failure more remote, even impossible. This time we have *little* children, and as any professional showman will tell you, the success of a show having children in the cast is in inverse ratio to the ages of said children, the younger the children, the greater the success. When you have a production casting one hundred and fifty kids, ages five to nine, you've got yourself a standing-room-only situation—and a king-size headache.

The one thing that makes these children more difficult to handle than the older group is their inhibitions—they haven't any.

Such a lack gives a spark of spontaneity to the whole affair. On occasion, throughout the performance, the director has the feeling she never rehearsed these children—and in one sense she's ab-

116

solutely correct; their effervescent personalities change from minute to minute.

But let me take you back to the day of the Spring Music Program, Grades one to three. The principals are as they were for the Christmas program, the same cool, undisturbed music teacher, the same calm, unhurried staff going busily about its myriad business, the same white-lipped stage manager dashing aimlessly about (white-lipped, not from fear, but from the antacid, chalky liquid he's been imbibing all day in appeasement of his duodenal upheaval).

The scene is 9:30 in the morning, the day of the event. Our stage manager enters, bustles about acting important, swears softly as he finds the stairs pulled away from the portable stage, swears again as he pushes them back into place, then hurries about checking lights which have already been thoroughly checked by the teacher in charge of lighting.

As he moves around he murmurs about the inefficiency of fellow teachers, the janitor, the principal, and all others concerned with the show. He is about to leave the auditorium when he again, as at Christmas, feels himself to be a victim of hallucinations. As he watches, the stairs, so recently pushed into place, begin to move, and a head, seemingly disembodied, rises up.

"Good morning, Mr. Hannan," says the head.

"Good morning," the stage manager croaks.

Another head rises next to the first.

"Good morning, Mr. Hannan," says the second head.

"Good morning," croaks our hero. Then, "Who are you?"

"I'm Tommy."

"And I'm Tony."

"We're from Mrs. Bisbee's class," they chorus.

His relief at finding he is dealing with real people turns his fear to anger. "What," he demands, "are you two doing under that stage?"

"Mrs. Bisbee dropped her earring down here when she was decorating and she sent us to look for it."

"Why didn't you say something when I pushed the stairs back. Wasn't it awfully dark under there?"

117

"Yes sir, but we didn't find the earring yet, so we just kept feeling around."

"Now boys," says our angry stage manager, "I'm really mad. I'm going to report this whole thing to the principal. You boys were under there more than 45 minutes. Suppose you had gotten hurt. You return to your room but you haven't heard the last of this." As the crestfallen lads start to leave, the stage manager reconsiders. "Boys," he calls, "come back here a minute, will you?" They stand in front of him, chin on chest. "Boys," he asks, "did you hear me say anything when I pushed the stairs in?" They grin, a conspiratorial grin. "Did you hear what I said about the principal?" he goes on. The boys nod. "And did you hear me talking?" They nod again. "Look, boys," says our stage manager, "what say we forget this whole thing. I won't say a word to the principal, how's that?" They nod vigorously. "And don't you say anything about this happening. Right?"

"We won't say a word, Mr. Hannan. We won't even tell anybody you called the stairs a son of a . . ."

"O.K., boys," the manager interrupts, "back to your classroom, and remember, not a word."

"No sir," they call as they scamper out of the room to spread the tale.

It's a long-standing rule that spring school affairs be held on a hot night. Only the most unthinking defiers of tradition would attempt to put on a graduation or play on any other but a hot night. Equally sacred is the architectural custom of never providing school auditoriums with proper cross ventilation. Combine these two inviolate rules with the natural tendency of the human body to give off British thermal units and you have a sticky situation, soon made more severe by six cases of upset stomachs in the audience.

In the dressing room, pandemonium might well be said to be reigning, and not a little of the disorder and uproar emanates from our all-worrying stage manager, who constantly harries the poor teachers to "line up to go on stage" twenty-five minutes before their entrance cues. He also helps the children by grasping them by the arm, looking them straight in the eye and muttering, "Are you nervous?", thereby turning every knee to jelly. Eventually, no matter how successful the stage manager's delaying tactics have been, the children are on and it is there that the true mettle of the music teacher is tested.

The opening chord is struck, a small figure steps forward, and everyone in the audience, especially his proud parents who up to this time didn't even know he had any lines, lean to catch his words. No need to lean, his voice carries well, "I GOTTA GO TO THE BATH-ROOM," he says. He makes it but his friend who "didn't feel good" doesn't and the janitor is rushed onstage to the thunderous applause of an appreciative audience. So it goes throughout the performance.

In the middle of the square dance, one lad stops to tie his sneaker. (He was specifically told to wear shoes.) During one session of animated "singing" a little lady decides to sit down. When motioned to stand, she shakes her head and says, "I'm sick of standing. I'm tired."

The triangle player in the rhythm band has lost his striker and tries desperately all through the number to tell the music teacher his troubles. She does a fine job of ignoring him but the audience, not having her college training, laughs itself sick.

But soon the show is over and sure enough we have another resounding success on our hands. Congratulations are exchanged right and left and there is some talk of doing the whole thing again. This rumor is traced to an exuberant and hammy kindergarten child and is quickly squelched.

The lights in the auditorium are dim and his figure is barely visible. He sits in the front row. In one hand he holds a bottle of chalky white antacid and in the other a small bottle of some amber-colored liquid. He sips alternately at the two bottles. When both are empty he lurches to his feet and makes his way onto the stage. Once there, he addresses the vanished audience. "Ladies and gentlemen, I want you to know that this whole damn thing occurred on Friday, the thirteenth." That's Show Biz.

Spring

Spring is a time of beauty, of green grass, beautiful flowers, and blue skies. Spring is a time of reawakening, of moods varying from gloom to gladness. It is a time of restlessness, a time of peace, and a time when teachers really begin to earn their money. Kids, recharged by balmy breezes and bright sunlight, seem to undergo a mysterious change. Girls, who up to now have been models of decorum, suddenly begin to pass notes to boys. Boys who seemed peaceful are changed overnight into pugilists. Frilly dresses, bright hair ribbons, bloody noses, and black eyes appear on the playground.

In the spring, the playground becomes a seething mass of boys chasing girls, girls chasing boys, groups of boys chasing a single girl, groups of girls chasing a single boy. At first you may mistake this for a game of tag but careful attention to the pattern of the game will make one thing clear—there is no pattern. It's just a chase, a wild running which somehow is tied up with spring and boys and girls. Here in its most rudimentary form is replayed the age-old game, the preparation for life. Eventually you will find that the original haphazard chasing has changed. Now it's always boys chasing the girls and, you know, the girls always get caught.

The naïve teacher, unaware of what's taking place before his eyes, will become deeply concerned over a large group of boys chasing one girl, especially since that girl will be screaming as she runs. Inevitably, in an attempt to preserve some semblance of chivalry, he will stop the chase, scold the boys and send the girl on her way—brokenhearted.

What this dumb teacher has failed to notice is that the girl he so gallantly saved was in a fair way to breaking the playground record of the boys-chase-a-girl game. Up to the moment of the teacher's ill-timed intervention, she had tied the record, having eight boys in her entourage, but even more important, two others were about to join when Big Mouth came along. No wonder the

120

poor kid's crying. Her bid for the title, Queen of the Playground, has just been nipped in the bud.

Other signs are manifest. Take hair pulling for example. This, of course, is a throwback to Neanderthal times when man showed his love for a woman by dragging her home by the coiffure. So, while the girls might protest loudly about having their hair pulled, the teacher shouldn't become overconcerned. Remember, it's the ones who don't have their hair pulled who are the unhappiest.

The Fight

There are all kinds of fights: gang fights, snowball fights, rock fights, and of course, that person-to-person conflict, the fist fight. Fights are forbidden on the school ground ostensibly to protect the children from harm, but really, I believe, to protect the health of the teachers who must stop them.

Picture this. You emerge from the building to go on yard duty. The day is beautiful, spring is here, the sky is blue, and the air— the air is rent with the excited cries of children gathered around two combatants slugging it out for the favor of the demure little blonde leading the nonpartisan cheering section. The cheering section doesn't care who wins, it's the fight that counts.

Of course, it is the teacher's duty to break up the melee, so you do. You make the usual fruitless inquiry into the reasons for the tussle. Conflicting stories emerge—not an unlooked-for development (I have never broken up a fight in which one party was clearly and admittedly to blame). Then comes the ritual. First the lecture by the teacher on the futility of fighting. Then the apology, one to the other. Finally the traditional handshake and the fracas is at an end.

Feeling like Solomon you then stroll to the lower end of the playground, turn, and behold the same two pugilists, so recently pledged to undying friendship, or at least to civilized behavior, back at the fray. Bursting into a monumental rage and a dead run simultaneously, you charge down on the battlers, grasp a neck in each hand, and tote them bodily into the office. Too breathless to press charges, you stagger out into the fresh air and collapse under the nearest tree, bleeding from the nose.

At first you pass this off as a mere hemorrhage of the brain induced by overexertion. As calm returns, however, you begin to remember happenings overlooked in the heat of battle. A flying fist at the bridge of the nose, a sharp kick in the ankle, a butt to the stomach. In the final analysis you, the peacemaker, absorbed more blows than either of the two gladiators. Let's go back over the entire scene and point out the mistakes made.

Breaking up the fight was a necessary action and one that couldn't be avoided. The first mistake was in making the kids shake hands. Allowed to cool off in their own time, they would have soon forgotten the incident. But, forced to humiliate themselves by shaking hands with the enemy of the moment, their antagonism is reborn. Shaking hands is a gesture reserved for reception lines and prize fighters.

The next mistake was complacency. Confident that his stern lecture had carried home, our bumbling teacher had turned his back on a smoldering ember which burst into flame as soon as he was far enough away. Even under ideal circumstances a lecture is only 22 per cent effective. Heard through a raging sea of anger this effectiveness drops to nearly zero (figures supplied by the Hannan Educational Minutia Research Bureau). At this point some sort of positive action is called for. It appears to be a punishment but is really a method of changing the focus of anger to the teacher. What our unsophisticated young friend should have done was put the two kids to work picking up all the popsicle sticks on the playground. And his mistakes didn't end there. He committed another grave *faux pas*. HE RAN!

The only time a schoolteacher should run is when the Superintendent of Schools calls. At all other times you walk, no matter how dire the emergency. The reason for this is plain. If you run all the children around you will enter into the spirit of things and join in the race. This means that every child in the area gathers at the scene of action, the one place you don't want them.

122

His raging anger was another error. It's all right to pretend to be angry but being really angry every time the provocation arises is detrimental to health as is running, carrying small boys by their scruffs, and placing yourself in the vicinity of flying fists (it is this combination of reasons that makes me feel the anti-fight rule is a teacher rather than a pupil health measure).

Notwithstanding, a teacher is duty bound to break up a fight, and if the above teacher used all the wrong techniques what then are the right ones? Let's repeat this same scene with an experienced teacher.

It opens with our hero sprawled alertly on the bench under the maple tree, dozing behind his sunglasses. Even so, being an old hand at this game, he is the first to see the fight break out and immediately swings into the first step of his technique—he ignores it, pretending he can't see that far. Besides, he knows that within the next minute and a half at least three small girls will run up to tell him breathlessly that Angelo and Rudy are fighting.

After the third alarm, our teacher arises and wends his way toward the arena, quickening his pace if a stranglehold is turning one face purple, but NEVER, NEVER running. "O.K., break it up," he says in a calm voice and they spring apart without argument. "Now, what was this fight all about?"

"He called me a bad name," says Angelo. "He called me a dirty punk."

"I did not," says Rudy. "I never called him a dirty punk."

Sensing equivocation the teacher asks, "What did you call him, Rudy?"

"I called him a dirty skunk."

"There you see, Angelo, Rudy didn't call you a dirty punk at all. You just imagined that he did. All that excitement for nothing."

"Yeah, I'm sorry, Mr. Hannan. Guess I didn't hear him right."

"Sure thing. Now boys, back to your games. The fight's over." You might feel that this kind of low-pressure approach is carrying nonchalance to the point of idiocy. Not at all. What our second teacher shows is a fine knowledge of boys and fights.

123

First, he realizes that with a few hair-triggered exceptions, kids don't want to fight and will go to extremes to avoid fighting. This was shown quite vividly by Mark Twain in *Tom Sawyer*. Second, he knows that the kids are more anxious for him to break up the fight than he is to interfere. Third, he knows that if he gives them time to exhaust themselves, they won't disturb him again by a renewal of combat. Fourth, and most important, he knows that of the countless thousands of punches thrown in schoolyard combat only an infinitesimal number ever are on target and those that so land do little or no damage. Occasionally a black eye will result, but on winner or loser a black eye is a heroic thing to be worn proudly and lost with regret.

The Bee

It is fated that in any warm month of the year a bee or a wasp will enter the classroom. When this happens you must do one thing before all else—stop teaching. You've completely lost the class. Although this may seem to be quite basic you'd be surprised how many teachers, teachers of great experience, will attempt to go on in the face of this insurmountable distraction.

Bees that enter classrooms are usually there through navigational error and are more than anxious to pick up their radio beam direction finder, or whatever bees use in such emergencies, and return home. The teacher explains this to the children using such homilies as: "If you don't bother them, they won't bother you."

Despite this injunction which the children seem to mistrust (perhaps because the teacher ducks and swings wildly every time the bee approaches), each child seems to feel that the bee is out to sting *him* and tries hard to get in the first blow. Then ensues a scene of waving yardsticks and flying books, each child seeking the honor of the kill. Such goings-on cannot be tolerated in a classroom and it behooves a teacher to be ready for the bee invasion.

There are of course many ways of handling this situation. One

124

method is the use of positive action—grasp the bee by the scruff of the neck and toss him bodily through the window. Another is to use a negative action—evacuate the room and call the janitor. Both these methods have the distinction of being extremely practical.

Other less drastic means are at hand and these have the added attraction of making you look like a really skilled teacher. The first of these is the scientific approach. The bee enters. Everyone's attention is fixed upon him. *Voilà!* an opportunity to study bees. In no time at all the insect books and encyclopedias are out and studies are being made of the aerodynamic shortcomings of the bee's bodily structure. Conjecture is made as to whether these imperfections are overcome by sheer will power—or has the bee discovered a new principle of flight? Stop motion photography is brought into play and the life cycle, breeding habits, honey carrying methods, and other mysteries of beedom are laid bare for all to see. This type of teaching is the epitome of opportunism. The teacher sees a chance for meaningful learning, grasps the opportunity, and carries the lesson through to its culmination. That's teaching and when these kids finish they'll know bees. Obviously this is a one-shot operation. Once you've studied bees you've had it, so what are you going to do with the next batch of bees that arrive?

I'm partial to the method I call the System of Class Control. The entrance of the bee is noted and one minute is allowed for looking, screaming, putting books on heads, and generally having a bee reaction. After one minute, the teacher calls for attention by banging the nearest child on the head with a pointer. After that signal no one dares even glance at that bee again. Not being a cruel man, I do allow a quick brushing motion if the bee lands on the child. If stung I will allow one loud yelp and three or four soft sobs (to tell you the truth I've had them sob eight or nine times and I've never said a word), and then, back to work. This kind of class control will bring you accolades from your principal and leads me naturally into the reason why I'm not too well liked by the children. The fact of the matter is: I AIN'T HERE TO BE LIKED!

Snakes in the Classroom

It will come. As inevitably as water runs to the sea, as spring follows winter, as small boys follow a parade . . . the snake will come into the classroom. As a gesture of love from a small boy or as a harbinger of spring, be assured that some day you'll have to face a snake. The time of the year to study snakes is, of course, in the spring. However, the truth is that the best time to study snakes is when one comes through the classroom door carried in a small boy's hat.

The snake must be made to feel welcome. I need hardly say that a loud shriek followed by a fainting spell is not conducive to a good snake-people relationship. The teacher must assume an expression of pleasure at the wonderful find, being careful to keep panic out of the voice. Remember, snakes are (for the most part) harmless. (It might be well, though, to bone up on the characteristics which distinguish poisonous from non-poisonous snakes.)

The first step in housing the snake is to dispatch your fleetest boy to find the custodian. He in turn will produce some sort of container to take the place of the hat. It is hoped that the container will be glass-walled as the movements of the snake form an interesting diversion (particularly during Arithmetic lessons).

There are, I've been told, two methods for feeding snakes. Snakes, it seems, prefer live food. That means finding frogs and placing them in the snake's general vicinity. The spectacle of a snake consuming a live frog is an interesting example of the scientific principles of survival in nature. It leaves the children in a state of gasping wonder and the teacher in danger of losing her breakfast. The second method of feeding is "forced feeding." This is easily accomplished. You grasp the reptile firmly behind the head with one hand and with the other you force . . . But so much for feeding.

Inevitably the snake will escape. It has been proven statistically that never has a snake deliberately been released. All cases of snakes appearing beneath the teacher's desk have been purely accidental.

126

Unfortunately these accidents occur with infallible regularity and the teacher should be on guard.

"The snake's out!" Before the echo of this cry ceases to vibrate through the room a dual movement will take place. The faint-hearted will immediately mount to the desktops, screaming shrilly. The remainder gather along the snake's path, shouting words of encouragement.

The role of the teacher in this emergency is a critical one. The female teacher might safely assume the position of bystander, remembering that no matter what fear may clutch her heart, no sign of it must cross her face. A confident smile and faith in "her boys" will (she hopes) carry her through.

On the other hand the male teacher must take a more forceful attitude. He should stand behind the circle of boys surrounding the snake, shouting advice and threatening to "pick the thing up myself." Only on rare occasions will he be called upon to make good the threat. Eventually the snake is retrieved, placed in its container, and the class returns to normal. The teacher, on the other hand, may not regain a sense of security until the snake has been removed from the premises.

It's Peashooter Time

Away with the robin, the crocus, or the first appearance of the Good Humor man. I, an elementary schoolteacher, will tell you of the true harbinger of spring. First will come the peashooter. Not that you'll see any little boy carrying one with him. Such foolishness would not be tolerated for a minute in any organization of pea shooters. Instead the teacher will notice certain signs which to the sophisticated tell the hidden story.

Walking through the yard one morning you will notice a crunchy sound at each step. Close examination reveals that the school grounds are carpeted with peas. Immediately a suspicion begins to dawn. Peashooter time! Already? But, no, it's only Feb. 16, much too early. Still, on more mature consideration you remember that the department store mannequins have been sporting bathing suits for over a week. Spring is fast approaching. Nevertheless, in keeping with your policy of never facing facts, you dismiss the peas as a natural phenomenon along the lines of summer hailstones or unexplained showers of small fish and go on into school. As you walk a stinging sensation on the neck informs you that the split pea shower has only abated, not ceased.

As the entrance bell rings, the signs begin to multiply. Several boys enter with arms stiff as if in a cast. A few enter with palpable knee injuries which entail never bending the impaired joint. Those with book bags stride by, full of confidence.

Upon entering your own classroom you are finally brought face to face with reality. Six small girls await you. Six accusing forefingers point to six small boys all of whom have suddenly developed a strong interest in grammar and are deeply immersed in its study. In unison six shocked females shrill six terrible words. *"That horrid boy has a peashooter!!"*

Your worst fears are realized. It's peashooter time and the battle is joined. You realize you are badly outclassed but you bring the six sharpshooters to the front. "Do you have peashooters?" you ask. Yes, they admit they do possess such an article but they didn't use it.

"Honest, Mr. Hannan, I never shot no peas at them girls."

"Why then do you have them in your possession?"

One brought his "to play with after school," another "belongs to my brother in third grade." The third, showing fine imagination, states that he bought his as a "birthday present for my sister in Junior High School."

The other three, noting that you seemed quite impressed with peashooters as birthday presents, switch their stories and designate their peashooters as birthday gifts for:

a. "My brother."

b. "My baby sister."

c. "My grandmother." (He was last and was hard put for plausibility.)

These six warriors are divested of their weapons immediately.

All ammunition is confiscated and as a warning the boys are sent into the hall to pick up "every last pea on every last staircase in this building." This punishment proved so fascinating that two others voluntarily surrendered their weapons in the hope of drawing the same assignment. They were told to stand in the corner.

These actions by a quick-thinking teacher are fine as an emergency measure, but as any experienced educator will tell you, there is no room for half measures when faced with the annual Peashooter Crisis. An all-out campaign of massive retaliation is the answer.

9:10—A small girl is dispatched to the office on the double bearing a message describing to the principal the situation as it is shaping up room by room and outlining the emergency measures already put into operation.

9:25—Headquarters then issues two directives, one to teachers advising them of the situation (that's a waste of typewriter ribbon) and a second to the children. In this, penalties for possession of peashooters are fully detailed. The consequences are dire, ranging from destruction of the article to letters to parents.

10:29—These directives are followed by a personal visit in which the principal reiterates the written word and also appeals to the better nature of all.

10:45—The school nurse "just happens" to drop into each classroom to talk about the delicacy of the human eye and the great danger that can be done by some "thoughtless boy" (I've never seen a girl with a peashooter) who blinds his best friend just because "he thinks peashooters are fun."

Under this barrage of pleadings and threats all but the toughest weaken and by now have surrendered their weapons. Wastepaper baskets are used to collect the ammo and the resulting haul is bagged and sent to the Federal Government for storage as surplus farm product.

Still there remain a few who will not surrender and must be trapped in the act. Best results here are obtained by teachers working in pairs. One, preferably with a tight dress, acts as a decoy. The other, hidden in the hall closet, pounces on the culprit just as he is about to unleash his deadly charge. Despite all these measures a few cagey old-timers will survive and it is not till the next spring campaign opens that the corridors and floors are entirely free of split peas.

The thing that really puts an end to peashooters is the advent of the water pistol. The tactics here cannot be as drastic as those used in suppressing the Peashooter Trouble since the consequences cannot be disastrous (unless you wish to consider the few who fill water pistols with ink or perfume).

Really, the water pistol in itself is quite harmless, and on a warm spring day a good water fight can be a lot of fun. "Why bother the kids then?" you ask.

Mostly it is the shrill screams that do it. It is traditional with little girls that they scream loudly if anyone so much as *points* a water pistol at them. This constant shrilling during playground periods set all teachers on edge. The nervous tension is increased by the never ending stream of little girls describing in detail the indignities they have suffered at the hands of the wielders of water pistols. It is most difficult for the teachers to maintain entering lines since so many are breaking ranks in the face of a watery salvo. Inevitably a teacher (or worse the principal) gets a spot on something silk which just came from the cleaners. This sounds the death knell for the guns. Wastepaper baskets are soon filled to overflowing with mashed water pistols which are bagged and sent to the Federal Government for storage (sometimes I wonder about our price support program).

In recent years the annual water pistol incident has been much harder to deal with. I attribute this to the startling advances made in the design and manufacture of these weapons. No more do we see single-shot jobs or one made of just rubber. Now they are hydro-pneumatically operated and are cleverly disguised as pencils, rulers, and apples for the teacher. I tell you it's pretty hard to find the weapon even after you've captured the offender. Just the other day I saw an unsuspecting teacher catch a shot between the eyes from what appeared to be a transistor radio. The owner felt that

130

he was unjustly blamed for what was obviously an accidental discharge. It seemed the weapon had a defective safety.

Now with water pistols and peashooters behind us we can be assured that spring is indeed here and you would think we'd assume a more cautious attitude when on the playground. Human nature being what it is however, you become complacent. You look back with satisfaction upon the Water Pistol Incident and the Peashooter Trouble. Certainly no one can criticize the masterful way in which the staff handled both those campaigns. Certainly those who felt they could defy authority are now fully warned and will henceforth behave with the utmost decorum. With such high and mighty thoughts coursing around in your mind it's no wonder you overlook a most rudimentary sign of another approaching crisis.

You, wandering in your ivory tower of false pride have failed to notice the increasing number of boys and girls who are entering the class with muddy knees. So with head held high you step into a large marble-hole and sprain an ankle. You have forgotten that with spring comes children playing marbles. You thoughtfully bang together the heads of two players who were careless enough to laugh out loud and limp painfully into the school to ask the janitor to fill those holes. I tell you in this business you have to be thinking every minute. Napoleon had it easy.

Me, Santa Claus, and the Apple Picker

Me, Santa Claus, and the Apple Picker! An unlikely combination you say. Not as farfetched as it might seem at first glance. Santa Claus, apple pickers, and I all have one thing in common. We are seasonally employed, or perhaps I should say seasonally unemployed. Santa and the apple picker, although working a shorter season than the schoolteacher and therefore having a lesser income from employment, have an advantage that the teacher doesn't have. They can collect unemployment insurance.

Santa and the apple picker have another advantage. When they

131

are out of work friends and relatives commiserate with them. "Poor man," they murmur. "He's been laid off." When I get knocked off it's a different story. "Lucky duck," they state. "Two months' vacation each year. What a racket!!"

In schoolhouses throughout the U.S. each and every year you may hear these lucky ducks preparing for their two months' vacation. Miss Jones who lives with her parents is preparing to tour Europe. Mrs. Smith whose husband is vice president of a bank is preparing to spend two glorious months on Cape Cod. Miss Smith-Jones who lives with a married sister is off to the University of Mexico for a summer course in Art Appreciation.

Then, too, we have Mr. Tired who has a wife and four kids. He has planned a great summer of travel—up and down the streets of his community selling ice cream. Miss Careworn who supports a widowed mother has decided to forego her regular summer rest in the air-conditioned five-and-ten in favor of a better-paying but more exhausting summer of tutoring. Mr. Roundshouldered who had the foresight to take a Civil Service exam will be spending his usual summer at the Post Office with all that great summer reading: *Life, Good Housekeeping, Ladies' Home Journal,* etc.

Countless others have planned exciting summers driving camp buses, delivering bread, tending bar, all of which are lucrative as well as educational.

So enthusiastic am I about this two months' vacation every year that I am founding an organization dedicated to obtaining for each and every person in America a vacation similar to that enjoyed by the teaching profession. I am calling it the "2 Months' Vacation Without Pay Movement" and its by-laws are the essence of simplicity.

Every employed person is hereby granted two months off without pay with the understanding that they will not work at the profession for which they have been trained. Also the time will be granted by groups: Doctors will be off during January and February. Lawyers will be free during March and April. Dentists have May and June. Teachers, because of their seniority in this movement will retain their usual two months, July and August. The rest of

132

the professions and trades will be scattered around throughout the year whenever they can be fitted in. I'm sure that there will be a great deal of overlapping due to the great demand to be part of this gigantic movement.

Now at first glance you may feel that this movement is all milk and honey and make a headlong dash to add your name to the ever-growing roster. But as founder of this organization I feel that you should be warned of the hidden pitfalls which lie in wait for the unwary. The most treacherous of these is the cold hard fact of economic existence in America.

Americans, you see, are charge-account addicts. It has been pointed out that our expenditures expand to surpass our income (Mr. Parkinson's law, I believe) and every American family, no matter what its income, is living over its head (perhaps we could except the Rockefellers, Fords, and others of their ilk). What I am trying to say to you members is that no one, no matter what his income, can afford to go two months without pay. You may scoff at my warning. "Just give me the chance," you say. "I'll show you what I can do. I'll live twelve months on ten months' pay." I'll bet you won't and for everyone who does there'll be ten who don't (booking that kind of bet may be the answer to my own two months of unemployment).

Another deadly pitfall awaits you when you discover that you can't make the two months without financial assistance. The question here is what to do for that extra money. (Of course, the teachers have a great advantage, the advantage of the professional over the amateur. We are experienced in many lines and are cagey about obtaining jobs which last just two months.)

You can forget the idea of working at your own job if the going gets rough. If this movement becomes nation-wide as I feel it will, your profession or trade will disappear for the two whole months. No matter what your qualifications, no matter how anxious you are to put your years of training and experience to work, you won't be allowed to do it. You see, you're going to be on a two-month vacation.

Now, I'm not one to form an organization, enlist new members, and then do nothing to help them out. No sir! My plan is to set up a certified employment agency so that those who wish to may be able to obtain work.

Admittedly the doctors will have it tough. Outside of a little snow-shoveling in the North there is little seasonal work during January and February. Oh, perhaps a department store might take you on for January to help with the Christmas exchanges. But February is a pretty dull month. I'm afraid you fellows may have a bit of a struggle. Lawyers on the other hand have March and April, months when plowing and soil preparation are under way on the farms.

Dentists, free in May and June, should be able to take up where lawyers leave off and continue with the spring planting. These months are also good for spring cleaning of attics and cellars, painting and redecorating and car polishing. Perhaps some doctor with a dentist friend might be able to arrange a swap, February for May, although such a change would have to be first cleared with the Adjudication Committee of the 2MVWPM.

You men in the trades who have September and October are really the lucky ones. By following the crops north as they ripen, you can keep yourself employed right through your whole vacation. November and December will find the office worker free to look for jobs in department stores, selling Christmas trees and, of course, playing Santa Claus. Now I must give you one more word of warning. You cannot expect to be as highly paid in this part-time work as you are in your own job, but remember this: It does you a lot of good to do something else for a change even if you have to take a 50 per cent cut in pay. At least that's what they always tell us teachers.

134